SECRETS OF THE FACE

Faces tell all.
This do-it-yourself guide to the age-old Chinese art of face-reading enables you to get to know the character, personality and fortune of people of any nationality, without even speaking to them.

For more than 2,000 years, the Chinese have studied the faces of everyone they met. Their art of reading faces is known as Siang Mien. It divides faces into:

- 10 shapes (which reveal the basic character traits)
- forehead (intelligence, memory, career, friendship)
- eyebrows (health, common sense)
- eyes (resourcefulness, trustworthiness)
- nose (wealth)
- mouth (reliability, generosity)
- cheeks (power)
- ears (sexuality, determination)
- chin (old age)

Siang Mien is fun. Once you have read this book you will be able to look at any face and tell whether the person is trustworthy, sensuous, jealous, kind, generous . . .

Lailan Young is Chinese, born in Australia.
After graduating at Melbourne University, she
worked as a radio and television reporter in
Melbourne before joining the BBC in London.
A spell with French national radio and
television followed in Paris.

   She now lives in London, travelling
regularly to China and other Asian countries.
Her articles about Asia have been published in
the *Sunday Times*, *Daily Express*, *Daily
Telegraph*, *Financial Times*, *Good
Housekeeping*, *Woman's Journal* and the
New York Times. She has made lecture tours
in Britain and the United States speaking
about China and SECRETS OF THE FACE.

   She is married to Robin Young, a writer
with *The Times* and wine writer for several
magazines.

Also by the same author and available from Coronet:

Love Around The World
Mouse Tales: All You Never Wanted To Know About
Mice

SECRETS OF THE FACE
The Chinese art of reading Character from Faces

Lailan Young

Illustrations by Jane Tyrrell

CORONET BOOKS
Hodder and Stoughton

Copyright © 1983, 1984 by Lailan Young.
First published in Great Britain 1983
by Hodder and Stoughton Ltd.

Coronet edition 1984

Fourth impression 1987

British Library C.I.P.

Young, Lailan
  Secrets of the face.
  1. Physiognomy
  I. Title
  138   BF851

  ISBN 0-340-34907-7

Printed in Great Britain for Hodder and Stoughton Paperbacks, a
division of Hodder and Stoughton Ltd, Mill Road, Dunton Green,
Sevenoaks, Kent (Editorial Office: 47 Bedford Square, London, WC1
3DP) by St Edmundsbury Press, Bury St Edmunds, Suffolk and
bound by Richard Clay, Bungay, Suffolk. Photoset by Rowland
Phototypesetting Ltd, Bury St Edmunds, Suffolk.

ACKNOWLEDGMENTS

My gratitude goes to:
My grand-master of Siang Mien in Shanghai and late master in Guangzhou; Seto
Chongchi, National Institute of Metrology, Beijing; Lin Kusen, University of
Nanjing, China.

My editors, Ion Trewin, Amanda Conquy and Mary Loring; Jane Tyrrell (illustra-
tor); Alan Chalk (designer); Brian Taishen Wang (calligrapher); Sissie Chan; School
of Oriental and African Studies, University of London; Society for Anglo-Chinese
Understanding, London; Charles Simons and Elizabeth Kerr of Camera Press,
London; British Airways' crews with whom I practised face-reading on flights to and
from Beijing, Singapore, Hong Kong, Australia, New Zealand, New York and San
Francisco.

Yu Soongkwong, San Francisco; Juliette Lipeles, New York.
Professor W C Foong and Tham Chanwah, Singapore.
The late Yee Gimhing, Melbourne, Australia.

CONTENTS

CHAPTER I
What is Siang Mien?

Faces tell all.

Everyone talks about people having an 'open, honest face', a 'careworn expression', or a 'cheerful countenance'. We talk about kind and evil faces, weak chins, generous lips, mean mouths, intelligent foreheads, and eyes that are seductive, wayward or mischievous without ever stopping to think how we would define the appearance that gives them a particular characteristic.

You can probably tell if those you know well are angry, happy, sad, hurt or tired by looking at their faces. But most people's knowledge of faces ends there.

Only the Chinese have made a thorough study of the art of face-reading. They call it Siang Mien. Dictionaries define Siang Mien as 'reading faces', 'physiognomy' and 'telling destiny by inspecting the countenance'. The truth is that through Siang Mien you can read the character of anyone you meet, and tell whether their fortune will be good or bad.

A number of eminent scholars have written about Siang Mien, including Professor Joseph Needham of Cambridge University who, in his encyclopedia on *Science and Civilisation in China*, refers to its antiquity. He observes that 'one very interesting outcome of physiognomy and its offshoot, cheiromancy (palmistry), was the early discovery by the Chinese of the practicability of identification by fingerprinting.'

The Chinese have practised many forms of divination for more than 7,000 years. Emperors and government officials called on experts to advise them about journeys and military expeditions, marriages, affairs of state and anything that might affect Man and Nature, Heaven and Earth.

Siang Mien has been important in China for more than 2,000 years. It has always been a secret, taught by masters to a few disciples. Books were written about it, and most were stored in palace libraries for use by the emperors. But throughout China's turbulent history of wars and rebellions palaces were looted and books burnt.

Most of what is known of Siang Mien today has been passed down through the ages by word of mouth. It has been added to by scholars and students of Siang Mien who have travelled the world to observe the faces of people in many lands.

Other forms of divination in China have faded in importance or become mere parlour games. Siang Mien has survived because, as the mirror of the soul, the face really does reveal a person's inner thoughts, intentions, and feelings better than anything else.

Chinese families in many countries practise Siang Mien without ever calling it by its name. My own parents warned against marrying anyone with small ear lobes or a flat nose.

Anyone who has been among the Chinese will have noticed the Chinese habit of staring. When the Chinese stare, it is your character that is being assessed.

The close relationship they see between your character and your face is expressed in their ancient saying:

You may strike a man's head, but never strike him in the face;
Even if you revile him, do not attack his character.

'Good' faces are not necessarily those you might consider beautiful or handsome. Someone may be ugly as sin, yet have a face blessed with good fortune. High foreheads, straight noses with plump, fleshy nostrils, thick ears with big lobes, rounded chins, and a mole near the top of the ear are some of the luckiest and most desirable features.

Siang Mien begins by identifying the shape of the face. From that the broad elements of character can already be discerned. Next the face is examined section by section – forehead, eyebrows, eyes, nose, mouth and teeth, ears, cheeks and chins.

Siang Mien also studies important moles and their significance, and special areas of the face which tell about health, wealth, careers, friendships, family relationships and love.

As always in life, faces contain contradictions. Contradiction is an essential element of the human personality. Siang Mien shows where the internal contradictions lie, and tests the strength of the features to determine which is likely to predominate in any given circumstances.

And so, to get the most from Siang Mien, you should consider the entire face of the person you are examining, and then – like a cartoonist – you can single out a feature that predominates in the face that interests you, and read about its significance in this book.

Nothing, not even plastic surgery, can alter the character and fortune revealed in your face. But what you learn about your personality from the study of your face with the aid of Siang Mien can guide your future conduct, benefit your career, and improve your relationships with others. By studying their faces you will understand them better, too.

In fact, getting to know people without even speaking to them can be done at any time, anywhere, by practising Siang Mien.

CHAPTER II
At-a-Glance Guide to Facial Features

This At-A-Glance Guide will help you speedily read character and personality in the human face.
Use this quick guide to identify the shape of face or type of feature that you are interested in. Then you can quickly turn to the pages that will tell you what it reveals about your subject's personality and destiny.
On page 1 the origins of this fascinating art of face-reading are explained.

FACE SHAPES

○ Moon face 40

□ Iron face 46

□ Tree face 42

△ Earth face 48

◇ Jade face 44

▽ Fire face 51

FACE SHAPES (cont)

▱ Bucket face 52

用

IRREGULAR
FACE 58

王 King face 54

▢ Wall face 56

THE FOREHEAD

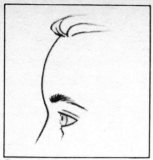

Smooth, rounded 61, 65, 71
122, 149, 163, 191–2, 201

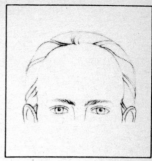

Deep 62, 71, 122, 149, 163

Wide 62, 71, 122, 149, 163

Shallow 63

Narrow 63, 64, 189, 192,
200

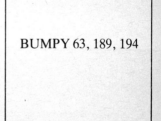

BUMPY 63, 189, 194

THE FOREHEAD (cont)

Flat 63, 65, 189, 194

Pointed 63, 189

PROTRUDING
65, 67

HIGH HAIRLINE
64, 197
LOW HAIRLINE
64, 200

Indented 65, 194

V-hairline 199

EYEBROWS

BALDNESS 65
WHITE HAIR 65

Ideal eyebrow 70, 71, 72

LENGTH OF
FOREHEAD IN
RELATION TO
MIDDLE
SECTION OF
FACE 67

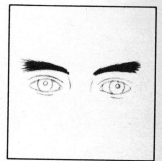

Brooms up 73–4

LENGTH OF
FOREHEAD
IN RELATION
TO CHIN 68

Brooms down 73–4

EYEBROWS (cont)

Hero's 74

Knife 77

Chaotic 75

New Moons 78

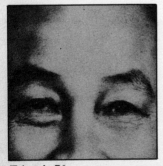

Triangle 76

Character 8, 78–9

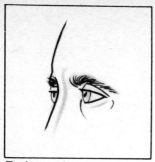

Eyebrows close to eyes
79–80

Vertical hairs at beginning
81

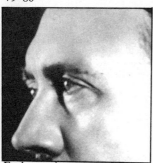

Eyebrows close to eyes +
prominent bone above
eyebrows 79–80

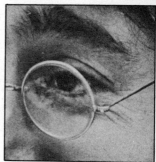

Visible eyebrow roots 88

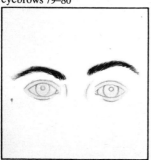

One eyebrow higher than
the other 80–81

Joining eyebrows 82–3

EYEBROWS (cont)

Very short eyebrows 83

CURLY EYEBROWS
+ PROMINENT
BONE ABOVE
EYEBROWS 86
EYEBROWS
GROWING OVER
PROTRUDING BONE
65

BALD PATCH IN
EYEBROW 81
BALD PATCH +
SCATTERED
EYEBROW ENDS 81
VERY THICK
EYEBROWS 84
THIN EYEBROWS 84
VERY PALE
EYEBROWS 84–5

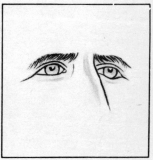

Eyebrow hairs
grow down 86–7

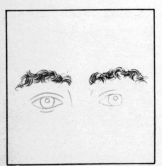

Curly eyebrows 86

EYES

Powerful look 90

The Good look 93

Shifty look 92

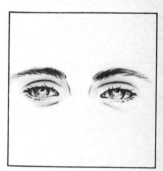

Sleepy look 94–5

The Good look 93

Sensuous look 95–6

13

EYES (cont)

Drunken look 97

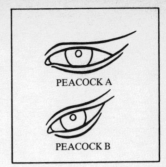

Peacock 100–101

Angry & mad looks 98

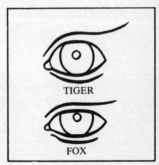

Tiger and Fox 101

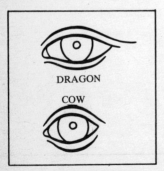

Dragon and Cow 99–100

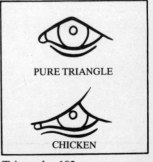

Triangular 102

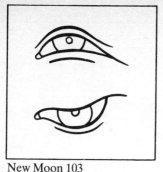

New Moon 103

One higher than the other
105–6

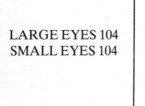

LARGE EYES 104
SMALL EYES 104

Wide apart 106–7

Eyes of different sizes 105

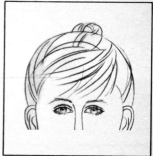

Close together 108

EYES (cont)

Slanting up 109

Protruding 110–111

Slanting down 109

SHORT-SIGHTEDNESS & LONG-SIGHTEDNESS 94

Deep-set 110

BLINKING 92

Pointed inner tips 111–12

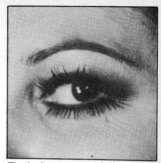

Eyelashes turn up 113

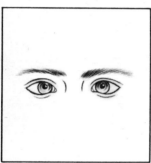

Cross eyed 112

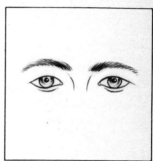

Single eyelids 114–15

LONG
EYELASHES 112
VERY THICK
EYELASHES 113
VERY FINE
EYELASHES 113

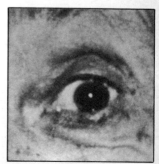

Double eyelids 114–15

17

EYES (cont)

BLACK EYES 115
BROWN 115
SAPPHIRE BLUE 115
EMERALD GREEN 115
MAUVE, GREY 115
LIGHT BLUE, GREEN,
HAZEL, GREY,
MAUVE 115
PALE EYES +
YELLOWISH 'WHITES'
116

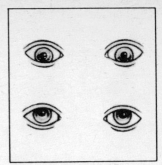

Three 'whites' 116–17

GREY 'WHITES'
116
BLUISH 'WHITES'
117
FOGGY OR
YELLOW
'WHITES' 118

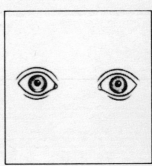

Four 'whites' 116–17

Two 'whites' 116–17

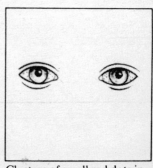

Clusters of small red dots in
eye 'whites' 118

Red lines in eye 'whites' 118

Indentation at outer ends of eyes 209

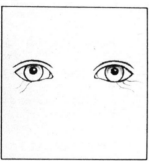

Lines under eyes 209

Bags under eyes 210

Crows' feet 211–12

SKIN UNDER
EYES:
PINKISH OR
LUMINOUS 209
SUNKEN OR
BLUISH (WOMEN)
211

NOSE

Best nose for making money 120

Straight 122

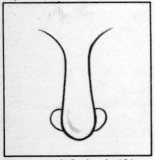

Very round, fleshy tip 121

**STRAIGHT NOSE
+ THIN NOSE TIP,
VISIBLE
NOSTRILS, GOOD
FOREHEAD 122**

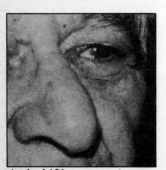

Arched 121

Roman or hook 123

One or more bumps 123

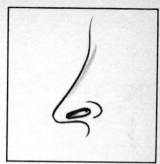

Long 127
Long + large nostrils 127

Downward pointing 124

Crooked nose 126
Crooked + pointed tip 126

Eagle (aquiline) 125

Crooked + round tip 126

NOSE (cont)

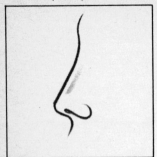

Short 127

High nose + narrow
prominent bone 129

High 128

Flat 129

HIGH, LONG,
NARROW +
NARROW BRIDGE
128

Childish 130

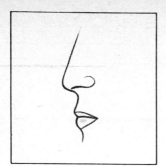

Thin nostrils 130–1

Plump nose 132–3

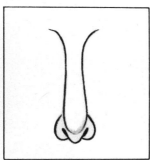

Thin, visible (viewed full face) nostrils 131

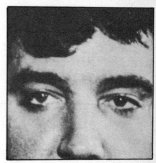

Wide bridge 204, 206

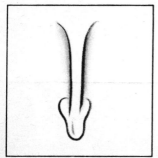

Thin, narrow 133

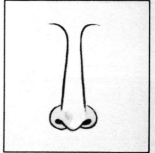

Narrow bridge 204

NOSE (cont)

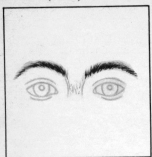

Hairy bridge 207

FLAT BRIDGE 204
LINES ON BRIDGE 205
POORLY SHAPED
NOSE + LARGE, THICK
EAR LOBES 164
SNEEZING 134

MOUTH

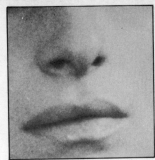

Best mouth 136–7

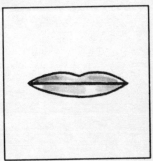

Straight, horizontal line
where lips meet 136–7

Wavy line where lips meet
142

Thicker upper lip 138

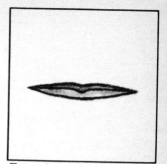

Exceptionally thin lips 141

Thicker lower lip 138–39

RED, BLACK, BROWN LIPS 137

Thick lips 140

Receding lower lip 140

MOUTH (cont)

Mouth corners turn down 144

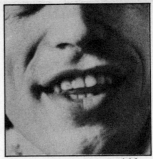

Mouth corners turn up 146

MOUTH BEGINS
TO DROOP 144
BIG MOUTH 137
SMALL MOUTH
137

Mouth corners recede into tiny hollows 147

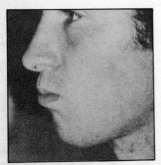

Pouting mouth 144–5

Crooked mouth 148

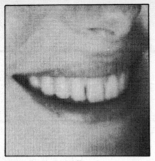

Good teeth 149

Teeth of varying sizes 151

SMALL TEETH 149
LONG TEETH 149
EVENLY SHAPED
TEETH FREE
FROM MAJOR
DEFECTS 149

Two large top front teeth
151

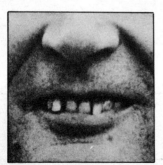

Gaps between teeth 150

Upper & lower teeth slope
in 151

MOUTH (cont)

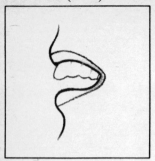

Protruding teeth 143

The three JEN-CHUNGS
152–3

Gums visible when
someone smiles 143

The three JEN-CHUNGS
152–3

THICK
IVORY-COLOURED
TEETH 151
THIN TEETH 151
VERY WHITE
TEETH 151
LOSS OF TOP FRONT
TOOTH 151

The three JEN-CHUNGS
152

EAR

Large ears 155

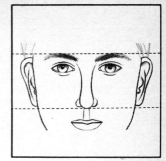

Best position of ears 157

LARGE EARS +
SMALL FACE 155

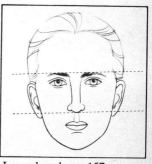

High-placed ears 157

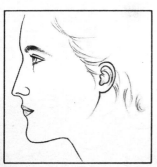

Small ears 156

Low-placed ears 157

EAR (cont)

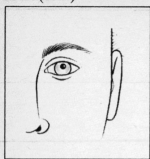

Flat ears 158

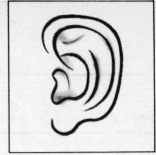

Squarish 160

Protruding ears 158–9

Long 160

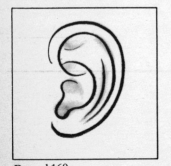

Round 160

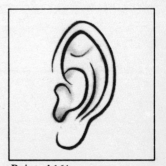

Pointed 161

THICK EARS 161
THIN EARS 161
EAR HOLES 167

PROMINENT INNER
CIRCLE 163
LARGE EAR +
POOR INNER
CIRCLE 163
LARGE EAR +
POOR INNER
CIRCLE + GOOD
FOREHEAD 163

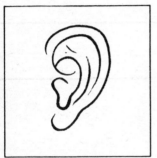

Markedly wider at top 162

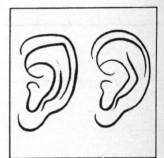

Sharp corner or bend on
outer or inner circle 163

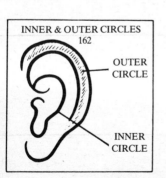

INNER & OUTER CIRCLES
162

OUTER
CIRCLE

INNER
CIRCLE

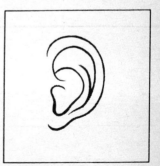

Small lobes 164

EAR (cont)

Small lobes + round, wide
inner circle 164

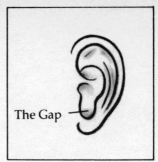

The gap 166

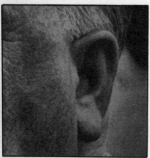

Large, thick lobes 164–5

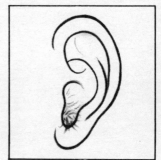

Hairy ears 167

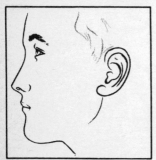

Lobe protrudes & slants
towards mouth 166

CHEEKS & CHEEKBONES

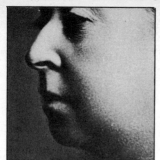

Rounded cheeks 168–71

Prominent cheekbones +
sunken cheeks + strong jaw 171

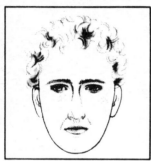

Lean, low or flat 169, 173

Prominent cheekbones +
very pointed chin 172

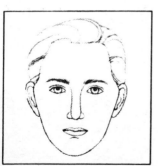

Cheekbones widest part of
face 171

**HIGH CHEEKBONES
168, 172
SHARP, HIGH
CHEEKBONES
POINTING
UPWARDS 172
HIGH CHEEKBONES
+ VERY SUNKEN
CHEEKS 172
DARK GLISTENING
CHEEKS 170**

CHEEKS ETC. (cont)

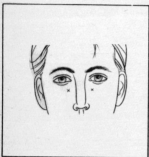

Lines across cheekbone 175

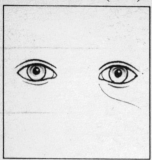

Sunken areas marked 'X'
174

CHIN

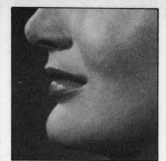

Sticks out/protrudes 177

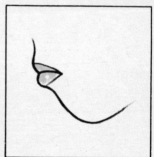

Receding 178

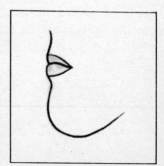

Smooth, round 177, 178

Square 177, 178

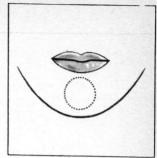

Fleshy circle 179

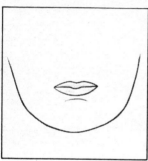

Wide 177

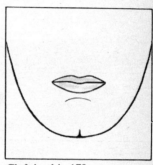

Cleft in chin 179

Small indents below mouth corners 178

MOLES

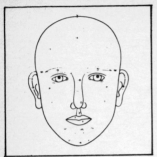

REGIONS

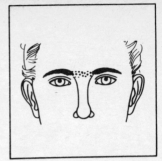

The Worry Crease 190

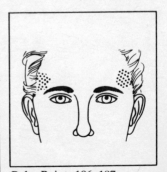

Career region 186, 187, 192–4

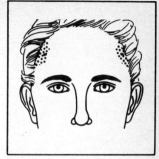

Parental region 186, 187, 201–3

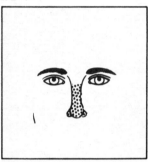

Wealth region 186, 187, 195–6

Health & Energy region 186, 187, 204–7

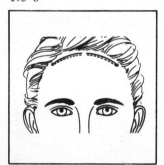

Friendship region 186, 187, 197–200

Love region 186, 187, 208–12

TEN FAMOUS FACES

The Queen Mother 214–15

Elizabeth Taylor 220–1

Princess Diana 216–17

Joan Collins 222–3

Margaret Thatcher 218–19

Paul McCartney 224–5

Paul Newman 226–7

Larry Hagman 232–3

Ronald Reagan 228–9

John McEnroe 230–1

CHAPTER III
The Face Shapes

Many faces are easily recognisable, fitting neatly into one of the eleven types described in this chapter. They can be identified at a glance. But some faces are combinations of two or, occasionally, three shapes. Combination faces take some of the qualities – good and bad – of each shape with which they are associated.

By using the At-a-Glance Guide on page 4 start first with your own face, then try to identify the face shapes of relatives, friends, and strangers. (And if someone you are observing has a beard, moustache, fringe, or hair masking the forehead or cheeks you must mentally brush aside the hairy bits.)

Never has there been a better reason to stare at people.

Moon Face ◯

The Moon face lacks a prominent bone structure, its roundness and curves the result of soft flesh.

To many, a Moon face reminds them of plumpness. In Siang Mien, however, the moon is one of the wonders of the universe. But before you decide that *your* face is round after all, let it be said that this face also has a number of problems.

Siang Mien sometimes compares the Moon face to water,

for as water can change course and fit into any shape so, too, can those with Moon faces adapt to situations and conditions. Even today some Chinese believe in an ancient folk tale in which a miraculous hare, which knows the secret of immortality, lives on the moon which is made of water.

Because of a tendency to be overweight, Moon people prefer mental to physical activities, and many are lazy. Some are greedy, too, and there is a famous Chinese story originating in the Ming dynasty, which can appropriately be told to any greedy Moon-faced person with a sense of humour.

The story tells of a poor man who met an old friend who had become an immortal. After hearing his friend complain about his poverty, the immortal pointed his finger at a brick, which turned instantly into gold. He gave it to his poor friend.

DENG XIAOPENG – MOON FACE

41

When the poor man said he needed more, the immortal gave him a big gold stone, but still the man was not satisfied.

'What more do you want?' asked the immortal friend.

'Your finger,' was the reply.

Though a little harsh on those with Moon faces, Siang Mien character reading suggests that the importunate pauper was a Moon-faced person.

Middle age is more satisfactory for Moon-faced people with thick necks, whereas a long, thin, swan-like neck is a sign that special care should be taken over any illness.

Siang Mien shows that a sales career suits many with Moon faces. Those who have a *full Moon* face find marriage a nuisance, even a bore at times, and also have doubts whether it is a good idea having children. Many have secret, erotic thoughts.

Tree Face ☐

There are more Tree faces, or combination faces which include elements of the Tree, than any other face shape.

Like a Jade face (which we will come to next), the Tree gives an *impression* of length, rather than width. The Tree is about the same width across the forehead, cheekbones and jaw, and so the sides of the face are straight. Of the two, it is the Jade face which has the more prominent cheekbones.

Tree-worship was already practised in China when Siang Mien was formulated, and there are stories in Chinese literature about trees that cried aloud with pain when they were cut down. As trees have knots, so a Tree face more readily reveals suffering than any other type.

Siang Mien shows that, like trees, those with Tree faces are able to weather storms, spreading their branches to protect their dependants and territories.

Like Jade, those with Tree faces are naturally inclined to be assertive, even belligerent. According to Siang Mien, these tendencies are sometimes repressed, but if they are

SHAH OF IRAN – TREE FACE

released Tree people discover in themselves inventiveness and resourcefulness that few would suspect. It is like a tree breaking into blossom.

But, one should not expect anyone with a Tree face to acknowledge, or repay, favours. Trees develop slowly but steadily, in their own good time.

Relationships with the family can be marred by petty aggravations, especially if the Tree-faced person feels cornered in a boring or unrewarding job. It is like being trapped, or closed in, in a dark and overcrowded part of a forest.

Trees derive more satisfaction if they are able to lead, rather than be led. The tree that is pruned and trained is less complete than one which grows naturally.

43

Jade Face ◇

The Jade face is recognisable by its narrowness at top and bottom and its wide middle with prominent cheekbones. Indeed, it is the cheekbone that distinguishes the Jade face from the Tree face. Both give an impression of length, rather than width; but the cheekbones are more noticeable in the Jade face, while the sides of the Tree face are straighter.

Jade is valued by the Chinese for its beauty and mystical qualities and is seen as a symbol of good luck. Likewise,

AVA GARDNER – JADE FACE

possessors of a Jade face are likely to have fortune through their lives.

Jade is also very hard, and the masters of Siang Mien believe that possessors of a Jade face are tough and have a will to survive.

For many with Jade faces, early life is marred by being misunderstood or undervalued by others. Some are born poor, but memories of unhappy or difficult times act as a spur to make the most of every opportunity. Siang Mien identifies these people as self-made, and able to overcome setbacks.

During the Ch'ing dynasty General Tsang Kuo-feng, himself noted for toughness toward friend and foe alike, chose for his front-line troops those with Jade faces. As one who practised Siang Mien, he knew the strength and fighting qualities of Jade men.

Yet, despite their vigour, Jade people are sometimes very unpopular; many harbour grudges and make sure that, sooner or later, the culprit who upsets them pays for it. What they consider to be doing their duty with thoroughness, others might well view as egotistical pride or an inability to delegate responsibility.

The most successful Jade faces are straight. This is not the same as 'keeping a straight face', but means a face that, when viewed in profile, is even and regular and free from bumps.

Iron Face □

Iron faces are square. The forehead is the same width as the jaw, and this width equals the measure from temple to jaw.

There is nothing wrong with being a square where the face is concerned. Siang Mien considers the square a symbol of stability and incorruptibility, and in the time of the Sung dynasty the name of 'Man with the Iron Face' was given to a statesman called Pao Cheng. He was honest, selfless and dedicated to what he thought was right, but so immobile of countenance that he never smiled in his life.

Fortunately, those with Iron faces smile nowadays. As iron is tough, softening at high temperatures, so those with Iron faces know when it is time to be pushy and when it is appropriate to hold back. Rather than make a mistake, the Iron man or woman prefers to weigh matters up before taking action, but once their minds are made up they do their best to see the project through. Iron faces have many of the qualities of which top politicians and statesmen are made.

Siang Mien reveals that men and women of Iron cannot be completely ignored because their views, however disagreeable, are sincerely held. But their sincerity is tested when they roam from home; many marry several times.

Those with Iron faces who can make their husbands, wives, or lovers feel 'understood' and appreciated themselves receive the support – as likely emotional as financial – from their partners, thereby contributing to their general good fortune.

SIR WINSTON CHURCHILL – IRON FACE

Earth Face ▢

The Earth face has a moderately wide forehead, wide cheekbones, and a wider, square jaw.

Chinese legends tell of the chaotic creation of the earth from an egg which then separated, the light elements rising to form the sky, and the heavy ones dropping down to make the earth.

HENRY VIII – EARTH FACE

Siang Mien links the beginning of the earth with the Earth face. Those with Earth faces are aggressive, especially if their face muscles are firm. Most are ungrateful and are apt to be spiteful. Quick to take offence themselves, their own down-to-earth manner equally offends others.

This earthy, sometimes anti-social, behaviour results from a craving for knowledge. Being self-made people, they are in a hurry to advance in life. Their resilience is as admirable as their willingness to learn is remarkable.

For thousands of years the Chinese have admired scholars and those who seek knowledge. But the warning given by Confucius against the dangers of incorrectly applying what is learnt is just as valid today:

He who learns but does not think, is lost.
He who thinks but does not learn, is in great danger.

Siang Mien says that, if two Earth people of the same mind, and with the same determination and ambition, cooperate on a project, their sharpness can divide metal and together they can change earth to gold.

Relationships with a marriage partner and children are sometimes strained, for the Earth parent can be tough and demanding. Stubbornness, too, is a characteristic of those with this face, but providing they can admit to any serious errors of judgment, they can find that stubbornness is a help, rather than a hindrance, in life.

'If Heaven wishes to rain or your mother to remarry, there is no way to stop them' is an ancient Chinese saying which sums up to perfection the determination of those with Earth faces.

QUEEN ELIZABETH I – FIRE FACE

Fire Face ▽

The Fire face has a wide forehead and high cheekbones. It tapers to a narrow jaw and a long, thinnish chin. (The Bucket face also tapers towards the chin, but it is broader, and the jawline wider.)

Siang Mien compares this face to a fire: bright, sensitive, and ambitious. When fire takes a hold of something it spreads fast; the Fire person is quick to learn, the wide forehead a sign of intelligence.

If the hairline is set well back this is a further indication of brains. People of many nations also recognise this feature, calling someone with a high forehead an 'egghead'.

Owing to their sensitivity, those with Fire faces are liable to make mistakes in the choice of partners for intimate, long-term relationships. Over-sensitive Fire people can meet further problems arising from an innate suspicion of the actions and intentions of others: in short, it is difficult, sometimes impossible, for them to trust other people.

'If what we see before our eyes is doubtful, how can we believe all that is spoken behind our backs?' is a famous Chinese proverb which has particular poignancy for the Fire person.

Bucket Face ▢

The Bucket face has a wide forehead and tapers in at the sides. It bears a slight resemblance to the Fire face, but is broader and the chin and jaw are wider.

Though it may be unflattering to discover that one's face is called a Bucket, it is, in many ways an auspicious face to students of Siang Mien.

Life, for many with this face, is happy until a new time of hardship suddenly begins. With their background of temporary stability, many are able to draw on inner reserves of strength, giving the impression that all is satisfactory and well-balanced even if things are going badly.

Their ability to appear calm and balanced can be compared to the attitude of farmers in poor rural areas of China, where irrigation of crops is done by hand. By skilfully balancing across their shoulders a bamboo pole on which dangle two heavy buckets of water, the farmers – men and women – jog round the fields at a steady pace. Very rarely do they lose their balance or spill a bucket of water.

If those with Bucket faces are to succeed in life, early on they show evidence of their intelligence and astuteness. Some of their ideas would be brilliant, if given a chance to emerge. But this face also belongs to those who experience periods of gloom and bouts of daydreaming, and the quality of their work deteriorates.

Most Bucket people are kind, though it is difficult to know whether they act from the heart, or in order to be praised. They are likely to be proud, patriotic, and to have an awareness of their own importance.

Anyone involved in close physical and emotional relationships with them can easily feel rejected, for no-one is quite sure what is really going on in their minds.

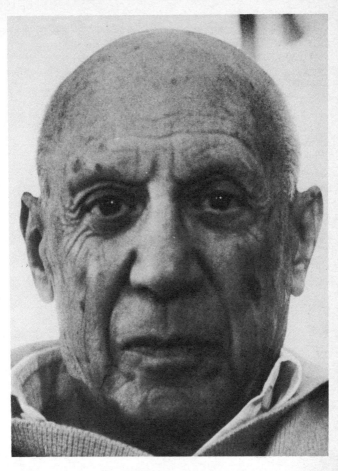

PABLO PICASSO
– BUCKET FACE

King Face 王

Siang Mien chose this symbol to represent the King face, because it is the Chinese written character for 'king'.

The King face is very bony, and the forehead, cheekbones and jaw are prominent. Not all the attributes of this face are kingly, but as history has shown, not all kings and emperors have been good.

ROBERT REDFORD – KING FACE

In imperial China, emperors were honoured as king-priests, guided in their actions by Heaven. Evil rulers, it was believed, would fall from grace by the withdrawal of Heavenly patronage, as described in a Chinese proverb:

He who succeeds becomes Emperor,
He who fails is a bandit.

This is the face of a leader, though many Kings resist – consciously or unknowingly – an inclination to lead, and are themselves led into bad company. Siang Mien warns Kings against truly bad influences such as the underworld of gangsters, informers and spies. Although this is not likely to happen to most Kings, there is never telling who a stranger might be.

Kings who accept the challenge to lead find that their gift is heightened by natural militancy, toughness, and persistence. They do not give up easily, nor do they suffer fools gladly.

Many can turn disasters into success; these are the rich ones, but they are also selfish. Siang Mien notes that even successful Kings are liable to a life of changing fortunes, so over-confidence does not pay.

Siang Mien cautions against spite. When confronted with the failure of a project or anything which is important to them, the temptation for Kings is to scuttle a relationship or project rather than permit others to benefit or derive pleasure from it. Siang Mien stresses that vengeful acts not only put at risk a King's fortunes, but also increase the probability of sudden and unpleasant repercussions: a sobering thought.

Kings like everyone to agree with them, and do not form close relationships easily. Life with a King husband or wife is often turbulent.

Wall Face ☐

The Wall face is much shorter than any other face, and also wide.

This is the face of a survivor, someone whose survival record can be compared to the Great Wall of China itself.

More than two thousand years ago, the first Emperor of China ordered a wall to be built to protect his state against raiders from the north. Built 3,750 miles across mountains, without the aid of machinery, it is the only man-made structure the American astronauts could identify from the moon.

Like the Great Wall, those with Wall faces can withstand harassment and attack, and their skilful parrying is victorious in many arguments. They are alert to danger, helped by the notion that 'walls have ears' – as often quoted by the masters of Siang Mien as it is outside China.

Those with Wall faces display a quick temper, impulsiveness, and an inability to plan ahead properly that causes many good ideas and projects to crumble. Siang Mien masters have said of those with Wall faces: 'Last night they thought over a thousand plans, but this morning they went their old ways.'

Given a choice, those with Wall faces much prefer to shrug off problems, and they do not like to think about the future.

As marriage partners, Wall-faced people can annoy and frustrate, causing their loved ones to feel that they are banging their heads against a brick wall. It is difficult, sometimes impossible, for a Wall-faced person to say 'I'm sorry'.

Women with Wall faces are tempted to wander off in search of adventure and fun with other men if they are not satisfied with their partners, or if they think a newcomer can offer them more.

IDI AMIN – WALL FACE

Irregular Face 用

Few people have totally irregular faces, but many have some uneven or irregular features. This does not stand in the way of achievement, as these pictures show.

DUSTIN HOFFMAN'S
MOUTH IS OFF CENTRE.

PRINCESS ALEXANDRA HAS EYES OF DIFFERENT SHAPES
AND ONE EYEBROW IS SLIGHTLY HIGHER THAN THE
OTHER.

In Siang Mien the symbol selected for the Irregular face is the written Chinese character for 'use', chosen not only because it resembles a lopsided face, but also because 'use' suggests the attitude of someone who leans on others, draining them of energy and spirit.

The unevenness of this face can be present in a number of ways: one side can be larger, longer, or wider than the other. The Irregular face can be bumpy, with a crooked nose or the mouth off centre. These are indications of emotional weakness.

Remember, though, that some facial irregularities may result from an accident or illness. These are to be disregarded; Siang Mien does not associate them with character defects.

Those who have studied Siang Mien know that to tread on the toes of anyone with a severely Irregular face is asking for trouble, for such a person is capable of wreaking awful revenge.

There is no doubting that the Irregular face is a sign of mediocrity, and, as mentioned previously, many of us do have traces of this face. Awareness of one's own limitations and problems is the best way of overcoming some of the shortcomings attributable to the Irregular face.

CHAPTER IV
The Three Zones

We have seen that in Siang Mien there are ten basic face shapes.

Siang Mien then divides the face into three zones:

1. The forehead, which reveals a person's mental capacity
2. The zone from eyebrow to nose tip, which reveals a person's luck or fortune and ability to overcome obstacles
3. The zone from nose tip to chin, which reveals how well suited a person is for senior citizenship and the enjoyment of old age.

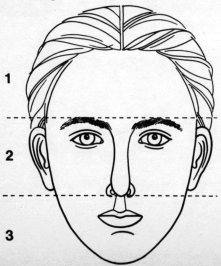

The influence of each zone is strongest at a different point in a person's life: the forehead has its greatest influence during youth and early adulthood, the eyebrow to nose tip zone during the middle years from thirty to fifty, and the nose tip to chin area from fifty through old age.

1. The Forehead

The forehead, according to Siang Mien, determines the extent of a person's intelligence and the ability to learn.

A well shaped forehead is the sign that a person is well endowed with intelligence. If the eyebrows are also good – defined by Siang Mien as long, even, arched brows that taper to a point – intelligence is further increased. (There is more on eyebrows in Chapter V.)

The best forehead is *smooth, rounded, and also wide and*

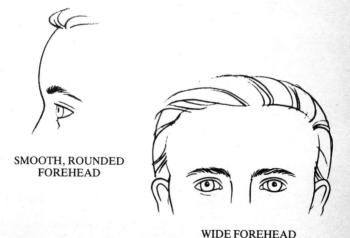

SMOOTH, ROUNDED
FOREHEAD

WIDE FOREHEAD

61

deep; that is, wide across the forehead and from the hairline to the eyebrows. Such a forehead is the mark of cleverness, clear thinking, and an ability to act decisively and correctly. However, not even those with the most superbly shaped forehead can make full use of their talents if the top of the head is flat, instead of rounded, or if their eyebrows are badly shaped.

DEEP FOREHEAD

A poorly shaped forehead is one that is *bumpy, flat, very narrow, or pointed.* A forehead that is *narrow and shallow* in depth reveals a disorganised mind and untidy thinking. An *exceptionally narrow and shallow* one betrays passivity; this person dithers.

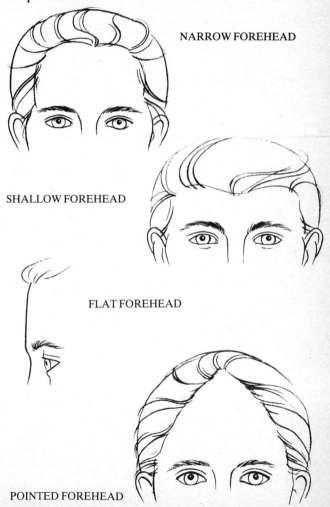

NARROW FOREHEAD

SHALLOW FOREHEAD

FLAT FOREHEAD

POINTED FOREHEAD

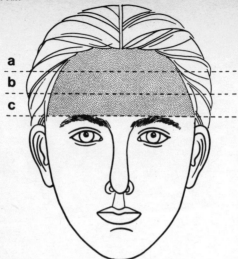

Declaring that 'clear knowledge is superior to profound knowledge', the sages of Siang Mien divided the forehead into three parts, each representing a different aspect of intelligence, knowledge, and mental skills.

The topmost area defines the faculty for logic and deduction.

A *hairline which begins well back* is an additional indicator of intelligence; if the forehead is already broad, the intelligence quotient can be expected to be very high. Even a narrow, pointed, or short forehead contains extra brainpower if the hairline starts well back.

A *very low hairline* that grows well down on the forehead interferes with a person's ability to think logically when under pressure, and has an adverse effect on the intelligence quotient. It also suggests difficulties with parents or guardians, who, even if they can assist, are not well disposed to give help, morally or financially.

Individuals with *low hairlines, narrow foreheads, and hairy corners* work harder than most, with little of the financial rewards they hope for; this is particularly so before thirty. These features are also warnings that ill health is likely to be a family problem.

64

The middle area of the forehead represents memory. The founders of Siang Mien observed that those with a *nicely curved and rounded* area here had the greatest powers of recall and the most reliable memories.

The memory area gives clues to other traits as well. Those whose memory area *protrudes* (more easily seen in profile than full face) tend to be quick-tempered, impulsive, and ambitious.

If a person's memory area is *especially flat or indented*, it is advisable for that person not to have a business or employ others, just as Siang Mien also subscribes to the common-sense Chinese rule: 'a person without a smiling face should not open a shop.'

INDENTED FOREHEAD

The lowest area of the forehead governs 'intuition'. Siang Mien notes that the most intuitive among us are those whose *eyebrows grow over a protruding bone structure*.

Baldness and White Hair are less important than the three parts of the forehead, but nevertheless fascinating to students of Siang Mien.

There ought to be no shame or embarrassment if a young person's hair turns white. Siang Mien discloses this to be a characteristic of superior mental qualities and – provided the young white-haired man or woman is of good character, as can be told from other features of the face – no harm can come from seeking advice from such a person.

Baldness is another matter, and Siang Mien associates baldness with sensuality.

Among the great bald ones are the three Sages – Confucius, Lao-Tze and Mencius, as well as some of the Eight Immortals, who gained their immortality through studying nature's secrets. Both the God of Longevity and Buddha were practically bald, and both have enjoyed popularity among the Chinese.

In the time of the Ming dynasty, some Siang Mien masters added their comments on baldness, recommending that any remaining hair should be kept as healthy as possible. Dry hair should be treated, they stressed, or leaner times would occur and might well prevail.

The forehead is a very important part of the face, and Siang Mien attaches additional significance to the Pulse Points and the Career Region, both of which form part of the forehead. (They are described in Chapter XIII on The Eight Regions.)

2. *Eyebrows to Nose Tip*

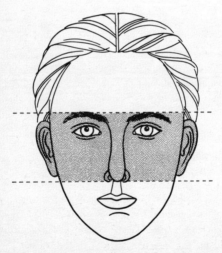

The most important contributory factors to good fortune and a satisfactory middle life are a fine pair of eyes and a good nose. There are chapters ahead on the eyes and nose that tell how Siang Mien identifies and classifies different types of eyes and noses. Meanwhile, by looking at the middle section of the face, it is possible to tell whether or not people have a good command over money, and how competent they are in controlling their emotions.

The most successful middle-aged adults are those who possess a good nose and good eyes. Those who have a middle section from eyebrows to nose tip that is *longer* than their forehead are persistent, and capable of overcoming obstacles and adversity. For them there can be no resting on their laurels.

Siang Mien demonstrates that a middle section from eyebrows to nose tip that is *shorter* than the forehead is associated with indecision and, at worst, defeatism.

Experienced students of Siang Mien note that if the middle section of someone's face attracts the attention first because it *protrudes*, this then is a two-faced person: sometimes withdrawn, yet aggressive on other occasions.

3. Nose Tip to Chin

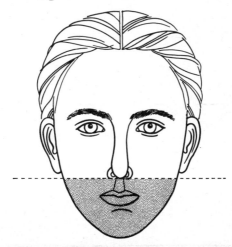

This is the area that reveals to those over age fifty how well suited they are for senior citizenship and the enjoyment of old age. The earliest masters and disciples of Siang

Mien chose fifty as the starting point of old age. To the Chinese, old age is a wonderful time of life, and as they are told from an early age that 'a family which has an old person in it possesses a jewel,' it is not surprising that most Chinese have no fear of joining the ranks of senior citizens.

There is a Chinese god of longevity, Shou-Lao, who is characterised by a large bald head and who carries a peach, itself a symbol of long life. As one of three gods of happiness, it is he who fixes the time of death, inscribing it on the tablet of each person at the moment of birth. To him, fifty is the beginning of a new magical era.

Those with strong *square or firmly rounded jawlines and chins* are more likely to adjust successfully to the changed circumstances of later life than those with pointed or receding chins. A further requirement for a fruitful enjoyment of old age is that the lower part of the face from nose tip to chin needs to be as long as, or longer than, the forehead.

Siang Mien also reveals that someone with a *longer forehead than nose tip to chin* measurement is likely to be an introvert, while the person with a *longer lower area* tends to be an extrovert. If the distance between the chin and the top of the neck is very short, this is a feature of a short-tempered person.

CHAPTER V
The Eyebrows

S iang Mien identifies more types of eyebrows than most people would imagine could possibly exist. Many people have two quite different types of eyebrows, in which event they take characteristics from each. Some also have two entirely different eyes.

This not uncommon condition has prompted the Chinese to draw proverbial distinctions between features on opposite sides of the same face: 'The twitching of the left eye and eyebrow denotes wealth; that of the right signifies calamity'. Hence the importance of knowing one's left from one's right.

As the eyebrows are more subjected to interference – particularly by women than men – in the cause of beauty than any other part of the face, it is sometimes tricky to imagine what a person's natural eyebrows were like before they were plucked or re-shaped by pencilled lines around, over, below, or above what should be their natural line.

It is possible, too, that the owners of re-shaped eyebrows have also forgotten what their brows were like originally. In order to find out about such eyebrows either they have to be seen without their make-up or beautifying aids, or you have to gauge – by carefully observing the eyes and forehead – what the natural line of growth is most likely to be.

According to Siang Mien, eyebrows reveal how well people can organise their thoughts, and whether their health is generally good.

It is true that more can be told about someone's health by looking at the Health and Energy Region of the face (described in Chapter XIII on 'The Eight Regions') than from the eyebrows, but thick eyebrows are indicators of good health, while thin ones accompany a more delicate metabolism. Chinese herbalists believe, as do practitioners of Siang Mien, the thicker the eyebrow, the better the state of the kidneys.

The *best eyebrows*, reveals Siang Mien, are shiny, rather thick, and slightly lighter in colour than the hair on top of the head. The exception is the Iron, or square, face (described in Chapter III on 'The Face Shapes') where it is advantageous to have eyebrows that are darker than the hair.

The *ideal length* is for the eyebrow to be slightly longer at both ends than the eye; the *ideal width* is half an index finger wide at the widest part (the finger laid flat); and the *ideal shape* is one that is slightly rounded at the beginning, rising into a gentle curve, and tapering to a point at the end.

ELIZABETH TAYLOR – THE IDEAL EYEBROW

In the famous Chinese novel, *The Dream of the Red Chamber*, which was written in the eighteenth century, the heroine, Black Jade, is admired for her 'pair of beautifully curved brows and sparkles in her eyes'. As Chapter VI on 'The Eyes' shows, sparkling eyes are among the best.

There is *one further ideal*: the *distance between the eye and the centre of the eyebrow* should be the width of an index finger laid flat. Anything narrower than this has an adverse effect on a person's career, while something wider can show a certain lack of coordination in thought and action.

The most systematic thinkers are those whose eyebrows not only have all, or most, of these basic good qualities, but also have eyebrows that are *evenly arranged* and have *visible roots*. But the eyebrows cannot be taken in isolation, for another Siang Mien requisite to clear thinking is a *well shaped forehead* – smooth, rounded, wide and deep.

Similarly, although a number of eyebrow types are inferior, many of the disadvantages associated with them can be tempered by having a good, or reasonably good forehead. Conversely, those with superior eyebrows but a weak forehead find that some good points are reduced, or cancelled out. There are more details about the forehead in Chapter IV on 'The Three Zones'.

There are many references to the eyebrows in Chinese literature, and paintings show that it has generally been fashionable for women to pluck their eyebrows and shape them into gently rounded arches. An ancient tale about eyebrows is sometimes told to young Chinese people interested in Siang Mien.

An ugly village woman envied the beauty of Hsi Shih. One morning Hsi Shih had indigestion and knitted her brows whenever she felt a pain in her chest. The ugly woman saw her knitted brows, and thinking this might improve her looks she imitated them. Her ugliness was now so horrible that people fled when she approached, and whole families left the village rather than face such an abomination.

Fortunately, one would need more than ugly eyebrows to incur such a reaction today.

At the time when the founding fathers of Siang Mien were formulating their theories about eyebrows, they noticed that there were many variations and that it would not have been accurate to categorise them purely into shapes. They remarked that other aspects and qualities such as thickness, length, and position in relation to the eye were as important to the understanding of a person's character as the various shapes themselves.

Siang Mien divides the eyebrows into eighteen types, some of which describe the shape while others are concerned with a particular quality of the eyebrow.

1. The Ideal Eyebrow

As we have seen from the description earlier in this chapter, the best eyebrow has the following qualities:

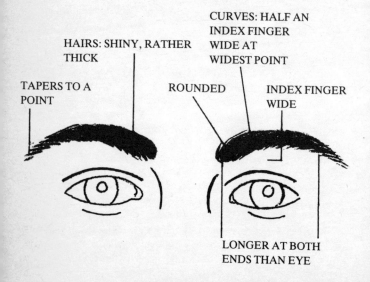

HAIRS: SHINY, RATHER THICK

TAPERS TO A POINT

CURVES: HALF AN INDEX FINGER WIDE AT WIDEST POINT

ROUNDED

INDEX FINGER WIDE

LONGER AT BOTH ENDS THAN EYE

2. *Brooms*

Siang Mien identifies two types of Brooms: those that are well arranged at the beginning, but scatter at the ends (called Brooms Up) and the reverse: those which are scattered at the beginning, but form a better arrangement at the ends (called Brooms Down).

BROOMS UP EYEBROWS

BROOMS DOWN EYEBROWS

Both Brooms denote a lack of drive and sufficient ambition to see a project or undertaking through to a rewarding conclusion. Those with the Brooms Up type of eyebrows give of their best in the first half of a project, while those with the Brooms Down eyebrows show more energy and interest in the second half of a project.

Siang Mien cautions the owners of either type of Broom eyebrow to be alert in their thirties against loss of money or a physical injury. If one's fortune takes a bad turn for the worse, little can be done to avoid problems during this decade, but an awareness of possible difficulties can at least warn against taking unnecessary risks.

The Siang Mien advice to those with Brooms can also be good for everyone: 'Don't rely on your present good fortune; prepare for the year it may leave you'. In other words, never take things for granted.

Those whose Broom eyebrows are very dark and thick are likely to be aggressive, even violent, though most are able to exercise enough control to curb any destructive tendencies. The masters of Siang Mien urge these people to remember that 'Propriety governs the superior person; law, the inferior one'.

Providing the rest of the face suggests a strong personality, someone with Brooms Down eyebrows could find success in a political or military career. (See also 'Eyebrow hairs grow down' later in this chapter, page 86.)

3. *Hero's Eyebrows*

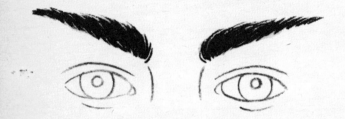

Hero's eyebrows are very desirable. They have a good beginning and a good ending.

Those with Hero's eyebrows are energetic, their thoughts are organised, and most are capable of greater than average foresight. They are ambitious and generally willing to help others. Those eyebrows which are especially long and sweep into a long, upward slope belong to lucky people who can act with confidence, safe in the knowledge that what they do generally turns out to be to their advantage.

4. *Chaotic Eyebrows*

As their name implies, Chaotic eyebrows go in all directions. They are also quite thick, and betray either confused thoughts or difficulties of concentration or, in the worst cases, both. Anyone with Chaotic eyebrows who is also impulsive generally lacks refinement.

Many with these eyebrows have a better physique than most people, but do not know how to use it to advantage.

If the eyebrow endings are badly scattered over a wide area, the years from thirty-one to thirty-four yield a number of unfulfilled hopes and aspirations.

5. *Triangle Eyebrows*

HO CHI MINH
– TRIANGLE EYEBROWS

Triangle eyebrows are often thick, and tell the world that their owner is selfish, but capable of courage when the going is tough.

Those with triangle eyebrows and lacking ideas of their own can usually improve on the ideas of others, thereby benefiting themselves and, if they choose, helping others as well.

Very pointed beginnings and endings of the triangle are clues to the acutely decisive nature of a person.

6. *Knife Eyebrows*

Siang Mien associates these brows with three words: clever, cruel, decisive.

**AYATOLLAH KHOMEINI
– KNIFE EYEBROWS**

7. New Moons

Most New Moon eyebrows are thin. Siang Mien reveals that the female owner of *thin* New Moons tends to be emotional and liable to physical passion, sometimes losing control of herself. A man with thin New Moons is likely to be exceedingly interested in sex.

Those with *thick* New Moon eyebrows are prone to bouts of hysteria, but strive to control these tendencies through fear of becoming social outcasts.

8. Character 8

These eyebrows are so named because they resemble the written Chinese character for 'eight'.

Early on, the Siang Mien masters declared that such people were 'more bright than upright', but later masters, believing that such an aspersion was not fair to all with Character 8 eyebrows, added: 'If the eyes do not look sideways, the heart is sure to be upright', by which they meant that, providing they do not squint, those with these eyebrows are of wholesome character.

A further Siang Mien observation of those with Character 8 eyebrows is that they are better suited as employees than as employers, though the masters of Siang Mien discard this reservation if someone has a strong chin or a well rounded Career Region (the part of the forehead described in Chapter XIII on 'The Eight Regions').

Character 8 eyebrows suggest a difficult period between thirty-one and thirty-four when a career is likely to receive a setback, but if the eyebrow roots are visible there should be few problems during these years.

9. *Eyebrows Pressing on the Eyes*

ADOLF HITLER–
EYEBROWS PRESSING
ON EYES + PROMINENT
BONE ABOVE
EYEBROWS

As we have seen, the ideal distance between the centre of the eyebrow and the eye should be the width of one's index finger laid flat.

Anything much narrower than this is referred to by the masters of Siang Mien either as 'eyebrows very close to the eyes' or 'eyebrows pressing on the eyes'. Such eyebrows indicate impatience and a tendency to fidget. Thin ones show that someone is likely to be more systematic – though impatient – than a person with thick brows, who is almost certain to be impulsive.

Coupled with a prominent bone structure just above the eyebrows, these eyebrows reveal an ambition that exceeds capabilities, which means that those with this combination often set their sights too high and, because of their lack of patience, are short tempered and therefore irritating to others.

In the fifteenth century students of Siang Mien were told the following tale. On the morning of his departure for the capital of China where he had been appointed to his first important post, a new official was visited by a friend.

'You must always be patient,' warned the friend, and the new official promised that he would.

The friend repeated his advice three times, and the official nodded in assent. When the friend repeated his counsel a fourth time, the official lost his temper and said: 'Do you take me for a fool? Why do you repeat such a thing over and over again?'

His friend sighed. 'It is not easy to be patient. I have only said it a few times, and already you are impatient.'

10. One Eyebrow Higher Than the Other

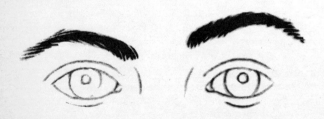

Almost from the moment they are born the Chinese are encouraged to honour their parents and elders. Siang Mien therefore attaches considerable importance to facial characteristics which give clues about one's parents and filial duties.

Some early Siang Mien observations about family ties are considered obsolete nowadays: one eyebrow higher than the other indicated having a stepfather or, as was more likely the case in China, a father who had more than one wife.

In a more accurate assessment but which still holds good today, one eyebrow higher than the other meant that a person is susceptible to emotional highs and lows. But in this instance Siang Mien does not consider this a significant character blemish in any way.

There are other aspects concerning the eyebrows which are linked by Siang Mien to the family.

HAIRS GROWING VERTICALLY
AT BEGINNING OF EYEBROW

If the *hairs grow vertically at the beginning* of the eyebrow this, said the founding fathers of Siang Mien, means that one has brothers, or sisters, or family relatives of the same generation who are not particularly kind or helpful.

A *bald patch* along the brow used to symbolise a sudden death of a brother or sister or, as interpreted by modern masters of Siang Mien, an emotional break with, or serious disappointment over, a brother or sister or close relative of the same generation.

A *bald patch coupled with very scattered eyebrow ends* warn of the risk of an accident.

11. *Joining Eyebrows*

For many centuries the Chinese considered scholarship the epitome of civilisation. Some scholars were as famous for their literary abilities as for their small waists (considered a sign of good breeding), long finger-nails (proof that their owners never had to demean themselves by manual labour) or joined eyebrows (brain power).

LEONID BREZHNEV – JOINING EYEBROWS

In fact, many mandarins – including young and perfectly healthy ones – were supported by attendants when they walked. Perhaps it was the Chinese who first said that there are those who cannot walk and think at the same time.

Such displays of lassitude belong to the past in China where even joined eyebrows are no longer considered auspicious. In fact, most masters of Siang Mien associate them with people who take offence easily and get depressed too readily, thereby creating mental traps for themselves culminating, at worst, in imaginary illnesses.

These eyebrows often belong to mean and unforgiving people. If success comes their way, it is unlikely before thirty-five.

12. *Very Short Eyebrows*

Very short eyebrows can be taken as a general Siang Mien indication that the individual is short tempered, sensitive and impatient. They are probably more impatient than even those with eyebrows very close to the eyes as described in section 9 of this chapter.

Some people with very short eyebrows do not like helping others. Siang Mien advises such people against turning their backs on others.

'The frost only destroys the solitary blades of grass' is a Chinese way of saying that mutual help will avert evil.

13. Very Thick Eyebrows

If almost every hair of the eyebrows is very thick and dark, these eyebrows belong to a person with a strong personality, probably an autocrat.

If the eyebrows are also square, this is a proud, tough and stubborn person, and likely to be bad tempered as well.

14. Thin Eyebrows

The thinner the eyebrows, the more reserved the person. Some are also lazy, clumsy and not at all creative.

Thin eyebrows serve as Siang Mien warnings of health problems, many of them slight, but nevertheless bothersome. This should not prevent such people from getting more out of life than those who, though allegedly healthier, engage in sedentary occupations and pastimes.

What appear to be rugged, or fierce faces cannot be taken at face value if the eyebrows are thin, for these are the clue to Siang Mien students that such people are not as fierce or tough as they seem.

15. Very Pale Eyebrows

Those whose eyebrows are *much* paler than their hair are not naturally fast thinkers, say the masters of Siang Mien. Yet, given a goal in life, they can achieve it on one condition: that they can overcome an inherent problem of untidy thinking and lack of foresight. But those who cannot ought to consider working with their hands in preference to a career that requires clear thinking and decision-making which affects others.

If the hairs of the eyebrows are not only extremely pale but *scant* as well, and if the hairs are thinly distributed, such

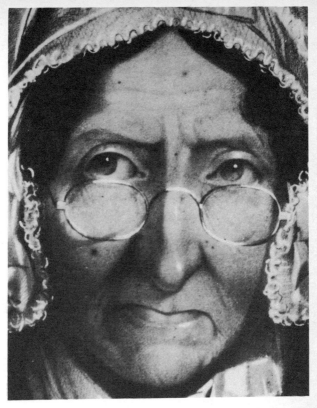

MADAME TUSSAUD – PALE EYEBROWS

meagre eyebrows are a sign that their owners will achieve very little in life.

The early thirties are not especially favourable for most of those with light coloured eyebrows and, as with thin ones, there are health problems, many of them minor, but irritating.

However, the masters and students of Siang Mien also subscribe to the old adage that where there is a will there is a way, and many with inferior eyebrows achieve considerable success, at least for a certain period of their lives.

16. *Curly Eyebrows*

Like many eyebrows considered imperfect by the masters of Siang Mien, curly circular ones intimate untidy and unsystematic thinking. They also suggest fickleness and a lack of affection, their owners preferring new relationships to established ones.

These eyebrows often go with *a prominent bone structure situated just above the brow*, in which case there is likely to be a setback in a career in the early thirties.

If the rest of the face is not good, that is, if there is a general weakness of the forehead, eyes and chin in particular, this person is likely to die before thirty-five.

17. *Eyebrow Hairs Grow Down*

Most eyebrow hairs grow upwards. Those whose eyebrow hairs grow downwards tend to be immature and at odds with friends, family, and often life itself.

If the eyebrows grow downwards and are also *dark and thick*, these could well indicate a change of fortune for the better after thirty-five, especially for someone who has chosen a military or political career. This is most likely if the face is a Jade or King type (described in Chapter III on 'The Face Shapes').

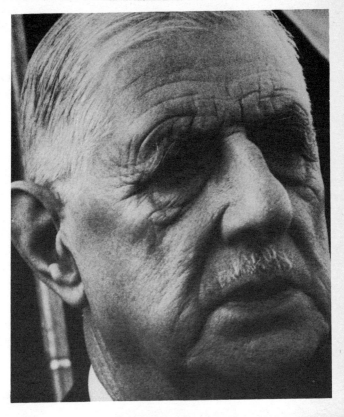

GENERAL CHARLES DE
GAULLE – EYEBROW
HAIRS: GROW DOWN,
DARK (BEFORE
GREYING), THICK

18. Visible Roots

There are aggressive tendencies in everyone. Some people are able to use these to advantage, but others go through life a victim of their inner conflicts.

JOHN LENNON – EYEBROWS:
VISIBLE ROOTS

Those lucky to have eyebrows with visible roots can, say students of Siang Mien, not only cope with unfavourable reactions to their aggressive behaviour but, on occasions, they will even earn the respect of the victims of their aggression.

CHAPTER VI
The Eyes

You cannot hide behind your eyes, only behind sunglasses. For it is the eyes that tell the world if you are powerful or trustworthy.

Because of their sensitivity, the eyes are very important to a thorough understanding of Siang Mien. In fact, instead of saying – as many of us would – that our ears burn if someone is talking about us, the masters of Siang Mien use the expression:

Eyes that twitch, eyebrows grown long,
Somebody's saying what you have done wrong.

There are Chinese who claim to be able to tell the time from the size of the pupils and whites of a cat's eyes. However, learning to tell the time from a cat-clock takes a lot of practice, and there is no guarantee that a Chinese cat ticks at the same rate as a cat elsewhere.

Siang Mien shows that, in order to understand someone's eyes, it is as important to observe 'the look', or power, in them as it is their shape.

This chapter examines:
The Look
The Shapes
Special Aspects of the Eyes
Colour

But first comes a Siang Mien warning – that it is easy to be deceived by your own eyes. The warning comes in a 1,200-year-old tale with a moral:

A man who lost his axe suspected his neighbour's son of stealing it. He watched the way the boy walked: just like a thief. He watched the lad's facial expressions: he looked like a thief. He watched the way he talked: exactly like a thief. In fact everything the lad did and said appeared to prove that he was the thief.

A few days later the man found his axe in a cupboard. When he saw the neighbour's son later that day, he noticed that the lad's gestures and actions were quite unlike those of a thief.

And so, Siang Mien reveals that a prejudiced glance is not enough. Judging character requires an objective and thorough analysis of every detail of the face. It is the work of a practised and unjaundiced eye.

The first thing to notice in someone's eyes is 'the look'.

THE LOOK

1. *Powerful Look*

Some people have such a powerful look, or gaze, that it seems to penetrate into the very minds of others. Some can outstare a cat.

In general, those with powerful eyes are able to assess other people and situations more accurately than those whose eyes are submissive, weak or watery, or not author-itative, although to be subjected to a hard or penetrating look or stare can be frightening and off-putting.

WILLIAM
SHAKESPEARE –
EYES: POWERFUL
LOOK

2.   *Shifty Look*

Those with a shifty look have difficulty lookings others in the eye, preferring to gaze at their feet, or anything, to avoid eye contact. These people are shifty or shy.

Shyness, according to Siang Mien, is linked to selfishness, because many 'painfully shy' people are so involved with their own thoughts that they are unable to open their minds or eyes to the wishes, needs, or even the presence of anyone else.

BRUCE LEE – EYES: SHIFTY LOOK

3.   *Blinking Look*

Some people blink a lot. This is sometimes caused by a temporary nervous tick, but very frequent blinking is symptomatic of mental instability.

Those whose eyes reopen slowly after each blink are less stable than most people, and where this action is especially prolonged the cause is likely to be neurasthenia, a nervous debility.

4. *The Good Look*

The Good Look is the best. Not only are the eyes clear, shiny and sparkling and therefore attractive, but they also number among their qualities all the attributes of the Powerful Look, already described in section 1.

PRESIDENT FRANKLIN D. ROOSEVELT
– EYES: THE GOOD LOOK

SOPHIA LOREN –
EYES: THE GOOD
LOOK

5. *Shortsightedness & Longsightedness*

Siang Mien reveals that neither condition has any adverse effect on character or fortune, except in cases where a person is too proud or conceited to wear spectacles or seek professional advice.

There is a popular Siang Mien tale about this.

Two shortsighted men were too proud to admit their defect. One day they heard that a banner was to be hung in a temple, so each found out beforehand what would be written on it.

'Look,' said one, 'it says Brightness and Uprighteousness.'

'The small writing under the large words includes the date,' said the other.

A passer-by asked what they were looking at. When told, the man said: 'The banner hasn't been put up yet, so how can you read what it says?'

Siang Mien reveals an additional quality possessed by many shortsighted people: they are sensuous and imaginative in their lovemaking.

6. *Sleepy Look*

As the degree of power in the eyes changes with a person's emotional well-being, it would be misleading, for instance, to assess people's characters from their eyes if they had just spent the last eighteen hours in a jet coming from the other side of the world. The 'look' in their eyes could easily be described as sleepy.

However, someone with regularly sleepy eyes is unlikely to be successful in personal relations, or in a career. Such a person is indecisive and disorganised, so it is advisable, when choosing partners in business or marriage, to think twice if their eyes have the sleepy look.

7. Sensuous Look

According to Siang Mien, anyone who has sensuous eyes has peach blossom eyes.

MARILYN MONROE – EYES: SENSUOUS LOOK

OMAR SHARIF – EYES: SENSUOUS LOOK

Chinese men are not fussed about being considered effeminate. What is in a name, after all, when peaches are synonymous with sexual success to the Chinese? More important to Chinese men is the wish to prolong their sexual activities as long as possible, so anything remotely connected with aphrodisiacs has popular appeal: ginseng root, many herbs, snakes, the antlers and tails of the north China grey deer, and peaches because of their shape and texture.

Thus in Siang Mien very expressive, alluring and sensuous eyes are called 'peach blossoms' as a tribute to the allure and beauty of the peach. Peach blossom eyes most resemble what might be called 'bedroom eyes': they are shiny, expressive and beckoning. They are the eyes of a great lover, someone who is terribly attractive to the opposite sex or, in some cases, the same sex.

8.   *Drunken Look*

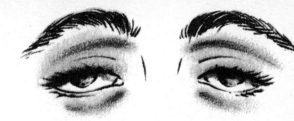

Of all the types of look identified by Siang Mien, drunken eyes are the worst. These are the eyes which resemble those of a drunk, except these poor unfortunates have this look all the time.

People with drunken eyes are weak, unreliable, some-times abusive, but worst of all they retreat into a dream world rather than face up to reality. You cannot expect such people to fight for their rights, or yours.

'Peace at all costs' is their motto, yet the world into which they retreat is far from peaceful because it is of their own making and is, for the most part, unhappy. They make disappointing friends and lovers because you never feel you really know them.

9. *Angry & Mad Looks*

Anger is reflected in the eyes and mouth. The eyes of someone roused to anger combine elements of dark fury, a steely glint, indignation sometimes, and often, cold hatred. Some eyes also bulge.

People whose eyes are always angry should be avoided. Many criminals have these eyes. Siang Mien reveals that anyone with very angry eyes risks an accident between the ages of thirty-five and forty.

Since the sixties, a large number of angry men and women, dedicated to political causes, have made news headlines. Some are genuine revolutionaries who want to change the world. Many have eyes that express the disdain, intolerance, and anger they feel towards governments and social systems and the people who support them. These eyes sometimes look mad, at other times angry. The look is very similar.

The masters of Siang Mien have never trusted the eyes of a fanatic, believing that their angry or mad look is more likely to frighten than inspire. And they have a cautionary message concerning those with angry or mad looking eyes: Do not entrust your life, limb, or property or those of loved ones to the care of anyone whose eyes are mad or angry *and* whose eyebrows are also poor. (See also Chapter V on 'Eyebrows'.)

THE SHAPES

Once you have begun carefully to study the faces of others and practise Siang Mien, it comes as no surprise to discover not only the range of different types of eyes, but also just how many people have eyes which differ one from the other. Such individuals take characteristics from both.

1. *Dragon & Cow*

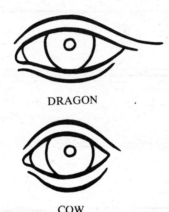

DRAGON

COW

The dragon, the most important beast to the Chinese people, was chosen by the emperors as their personal symbol of power. Not surprisingly, the masters of Siang Mien consider Dragon eyes the most powerful and beautiful shape of all.

Dragon eyes are large. They are more elongated than the Cow, with larger areas of white to the left and right of the iris. They indicate that their owner is innovative, with lots of ideas, some of which are good, others chancy, many hopeless. The Dragon-eyed person is good company, brave – without necessarily knowing it until put to the test – and usually generous.

Cow eyes can also be attractive, but suggest stubbornness. Smaller than Dragon eyes, they appear rounder because they are more compact.

People with Cow eyes are frank, but their direct manner sometimes causes offence. Cow-eyed people should be taken at face value: you know where you stand with them. They have a capacity for hard work, their output dropping, or poor, only if they are unsuited to a task.

2. *Peacock*

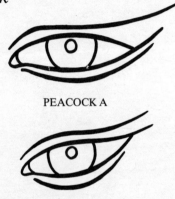

PEACOCK A

PEACOCK B

Siang Mien calls the two rectangular-shaped eyes Peacock A and Peacock B. Peacock A are longer and less slanted than the B type.

Peacock A eyes are associated with people who react emotionally to events and situations which do not appeal to them, or which they think are beyond them. They can be charmers, but if the object of their desires or needs – whether human or not – slips from their grasp, their jealousy can be disturbing and unnerving.

Less attractive are Peacock B eyes, which have smaller areas of white on either side of the iris. The characteristics are similar to the Peacock A, except that they betray excessive jealousy. The best way to control such jealousy is to act on some Confucian advice: 'If you attack your own failings instead of those of others, you will remedy your personal faults.'

3. Tiger & Fox

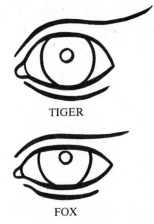

TIGER

FOX

The Tiger eye is superior to the Fox, for it is the larger of the two, and the area of white more generous. People with Tiger eyes see ahead and set their sights on a quarry. They have staying power, and should make good civil servants, local-government workers or policemen because, having identified their target or problem, they will persist until the job is done.

The smaller Fox eye is a sign of native cunning and, in some cases, dishonesty. This does not mean that a Fox-eyed person is never to be trusted, because the whole face would have to be considered before such a conclusion could be made.

The villain in many Chinese traditional tales is a fox which operates in disguise, tricking and cheating good folk. The Fox eye in the Siang Mien charts is noted for its meanness, so it is not surprising that Fox-eyed people are ungenerous.

101

4. *Triangular*

The larger of the two Triangle eyes is called the Pure Triangle and the smaller, the Chicken. Those with either can feel – with reason – that not many people like them very much.

PURE TRIANGLE

People with Pure Triangle eyes dislike anyone who opposes them or disagrees with their views. Many will brook no opposition under any circumstances, and with a single withering look – which could be said to resemble the hooded look of a crow – they can silence all-comers.

These people are capable of using, even stepping on, others to achieve their ambitions. Some Siang Mien students say that Pure Triangle-eyed people have eyes at the back of the head, so wily are they at manipulating others. This eye is particularly good for anyone attracted to a political career.

CHICKEN

If the eyelid droops over the eye, this type of Triangle eye is known as the Chicken.

Siang Mien brings to notice that Chicken-eyed people are nervy, pernickety and, appropriately, many spend a lot of time fretting and clucking round like busy hens. Many are interfering busybodies.

5. *New Moon*

NEW MOON

NEW MOON

New Moon eyes are, alas, neither beautiful nor good. It is to be hoped that those with such eyes have other good facial features to counteract them, for New Moon eyes denote dishonesty to an even greater degree than the Fox eye.

Generally, a man with New Moon eyes takes advantage of women or anyone he considers inferior. Equally liable to use people, New Moon-eyed women also enjoy brief sexual encounters (or would, if they dared), but settle down to a long relationship if a partner satisfies them.

SPECIAL ASPECTS OF THE EYES

As well as types and shapes of eyes, the student of Siang Mien needs to look for a number of salient factors, such as the importance of the eyelashes and the angle of the eyes in relation to the rest of the face. We begin with size.

1. *Large & Small Eyes*

LUCIANO PAVAROTTI
– LARGE EYES

Large eyes are better than small ones, being associated with happier people who, though sometimes too impulsive and passionate, get more fun out of life than small-eyed people.

Small eyes reveal that a person is uptight about too many things in life: too reserved perhaps, or too conscious of appearances and of what others might say. Those who come to terms with these foibles can brush aside their natural reserve and caution to find that personal effort improves their lot in life.

2. *Different Sizes, Different Levels*

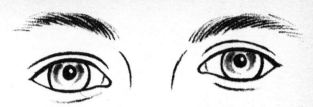

ONE EYE HIGHER THAN THE OTHER

When the art of Siang Mien was first developed it was supposed that anyone with eyes of different sizes, or one eye or eyebrow higher than the other, had stepfathers or stepmothers, but as the custom grew permitting men to have several wives and concubines, it soon became evident that not all the millions of people with step-parents could have these eyes or eyebrows.

ERNEST HEMINGWAY – EYES OF DIFFERENT SIZES

Now it is realised that eyes of *different sizes* belong to those whose fortunes are uneven. Some years are very good, some poor, with a span of mediocre years before an upturn of fortune.

When one eye is *higher than the other*, emotional ups and downs govern the fortune. Siang Mien shows that this is also true of those with one eyebrow higher than the other. Individuals with either or both characteristics are tough on themselves, sometimes setting standards of achievement beyond their abilities.

And so, instead of shrugging off bad patches or minor setbacks, as would most people, they overreact in adversity, blaming themselves for misfortunes beyond their control, and lack fighting spirit when it is most needed.

They also tend to daydream at inappropriate moments. Seeking to escape life's realities, they experience many crises in their lives.

3. Wide Apart or Close Together

Eyes set *wide apart* provide a bird's-eye view of the world. This ability to see life in a broader spectrum gives many opportunities denied to most people, but not everyone with such eyes can make use of it.

In *The Merry Wives of Windsor*, Pistol says:

Why, then the world's mine oyster,
Which I with sword will open.

The original masters of Siang Mien would have loved these Shakespearean lines and connected them with a favourite story first told in China more than 2,000 years ago and especially popular during the turbulent period of the warring states.

An oyster was opening its shell when a bird pecked at it. The oyster clamped down its shell on the bird's beak and held on.

'If it doesn't rain there will be one dead oyster,' said the bird.
'If you can't break away there'll be one dead bird,' retorted the oyster.

A fisherman walked by and caught them both.

This ancient Chinese story shows how important it is to make the most of one's opportunities. Here, both the bird and oyster lost out by not being able to see the limitations of their own abilities. Siang Mien advises those with eyes set wide apart to use their greater gift of sight to advantage, and to grasp the significance of what there is to see.

CAPTAIN JAMES COOK – EYES WIDE APART

Those whose eyes are set *close together* tend, like someone whose eyes are small, to be reserved and conscious of appearances. Some are narrow-minded. Others are introverted though they will deny it or may not even realise they are. Many such persons choose a career more suited to an extrovert in order to prove to themselves – consciously or subconsciously – that they are more daring and gregarious than they really feel.

Close-set eyes give an appearance of irritability that may be quite unjustified. More likely this indicates a fear of being left out of things, or of not being able to cope with a situation.

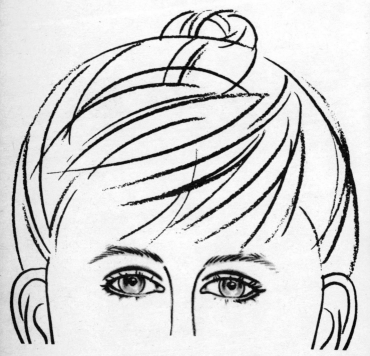

EYES SET CLOSE TOGETHER

4. *Slanting Eyes*

EYES SLANTING UPWARDS

EYES SLANTING DOWN

Eyes that *slant upwards* reflect pride and optimism, but too much pride if the eyebrows also slope up.

Eyes *slanting down* indicate a rather cautious personality, someone who looks and thinks before leaping. This characteristic is more evident if the brows also slope down. Many pessimists also have these eyes.

Siang Mien stresses that it is also important to take certain obvious racial characteristics into account when studying a person's face.

For instance, many Japanese have naturally slanting eyes, so one should remember this before deciding whether a particular Japanese person's eyes slope more than do most men and women of that race.

5. *Deep-set Eyes*

Siang Mien reveals that deep-set, or sunken, eyes belong to people who are withdrawn, secretive, or difficult to understand. Most of the time they have a tight control over their emotions.

Siang Mien advises you to be wary of those whose eyes are both deep-set and slitty. If necessary, they will stab someone in the back who comes between them and their goal.

6. *Protruding Eyes*

As we have seen in the 'Angry Eyes' section, eyes often protrude if a person is angry. Siang Mien students sometimes describe an extremely angry person as being 'so angry that the hair stands up under the cap and the eyes bulge like those of the Yellow River fish'.

Permanently protruding eyes are, reveals Siang Mien, a sign of hypersensitive emotions. If, however, they are the result of a medical condition such as goitre, this assessment does not necessarily apply.

Slightly protruding eyes are more acceptable to Siang Mien students, belonging in the main to sociable people who can mix with strangers without showing self-consciousness.

However, Siang Mien has advice concerning protruding eyes: though often these people are good company, do not tell them secrets unless you want your secrets to become public knowledge.

7. Pointed Inner Tips; Cross-Eyed

EDITH PIAF – EYES: POINTED INNER TIPS

A lot of people have pointed inner tips near the nose. In many cases this is an indication of uneven fortune around mid-life, which is likely to be caused by over-spending or misjudging investments or savings by a member of the family.

111

Extremely pointed inner tips are a Siang Mien sign that an individual finds it difficult to concentrate. Some are liable to fall asleep at inappropriate times.

CROSS-EYED

Finances in mid-life are also threatened for those who are cross-eyed. It is worth knowing this for anyone thinking of marrying a person with such eyes. Siang Mien would not go so far as suggesting that the marriage should be called off, but a Chinese proverb should be borne in mind: 'A great fortune depends on luck, a small one on diligence,' and if your spouse-to-be disagrees with this it is obvious that he or she should not be given control of the family's purse strings.

8. *Eyelashes*

'Eyes cannot see their own lashes.' The significance of this Siang Mien observation – obvious when you think of it – is the implication that people cannot see their own faults.

Though *long eyelashes* are rare in China, this did not prevent the early masters of Siang Mien or their disciples from admiring them for their beauty, nor from remarking that long lashes, though attractive, cannot be approved of unreservedly because they are frequently found on the faces of people whose emotions get the better of them.

Like most Chinese, the Siang Mien masters and their followers abhorred public displays of inner feelings, including expressions of love or affection, thus strict control over one's behaviour in the presence of others was, and still is, expected at all times.

CLAUDIA CARDINALE
– EYELASHES TURN UP

Very thick eyelash hairs further add to any emotional instability that may be present, and *very fine hairs* suggest a cool disposition for most of the time, but their owner can be ferocious if roused.

Eyelashes which *curl or turn up* without the aid of curlers or tongs signal optimism or passion.

9. *Eyelids*

SINGLE EYELIDS

Although single eyelids are more common among the Chinese than most races, Siang Mien considers double eyelids superior.

ALBERT EINSTEIN: A LOVELY TONGUE, BUT IT IS THE DOUBLE EYELIDS THAT COUNT

Single eyelids may be taken as a warning that a person is cold-hearted, even frigid, and are associated with those who have difficulty forming lasting friendships.

For many centuries the Japanese have shown an interest in Siang Mien, and it is fascinating to reflect on the desire, a craze even, of millions of Japanese women to undergo surgery on their eyelids in order to turn single lids into double. Japanese men do not mind going through life with single eyelids.

COLOURS OF EYES

Black is beautiful. This is not a twentieth-century idea new to the Chinese, but an ancient Siang Mien disclosure that black eyes are synonymous with foresight, decisiveness, and a high intelligence quotient (IQ).

Let us not kid ourselves, those of us with dark brown eyes. They may look black at midnight or on a dull day, but the test is in bright daylight, and not many people have genuine and permanent black eyes.

Dark brown eyes are superior to light brown. They signify a loyalty towards the family, first as a son or daughter, later as a parent who will, if called upon, make sacrifices for the sake of the children.

Light brown eyes are associated with the ability to withdraw unscathed from unhappy and unsuccessful relationships. Those who have them are not especially affectionate people. They may act in self-defence and self-interest, but they leave behind a number of shattered people, often unaware of the havoc or pain they have caused.

Intensely sapphire blue eyes, or *strong emerald green*, or *shiny mauve or grey* eyes are signs of an active mind. *Light blue, green, hazel, grey or mauve* are in no way inferior, but a person with pale eyes is likely to have to work harder and dip into inner reserves of energy in order to be outstandingly successful.

Pale eyes *surrounded by yellowish 'whites'* indicate a mediocre person liable to bouts of melancholy. A *circle of grey clouds* which forms around the grey eyes of a young person is a warning of poor health and poor fortune in middle age.

The *whites* of eyes impart valuable information to those who understand Siang Mien.

Most eyes have two areas of white: to the left and right of the iris. But eyes with three or four areas of white tell most.

Eyes with three areas of white have them on either side of the iris plus either an area of white above the iris or below it. Siang Mien advises against close friendships with anyone who has three areas of white.

While it is popular in the West to speak of 'turning a blind eye' to something, the Chinese have an equally colourful expression: 'to turn a white eye' against people means to disapprove of them and to criticise them behind their backs.

If the upper eye – that is, *above the iris* – is white, this reveals that a person is hypersensitive, takes offence easily, is self-centred and, if roused, can be quite brutish.

A person with white *below the iris* is oversensitive, and tends to be self-conscious, but is more likable than someone with white showing in the upper eye.

With *four whites* showing, the iris is like an island surrounded by a sea of white. This is the eye of someone difficult to ignore. With a tendency to be scathing when annoyed, those with four whites are bright, decisive, efficient, and good at managing people – the stuff of which good executives should be made. But four-whites people are rare, so the wrong people get many of the top jobs, a sorry tale for industry and commerce all over the world.

All those with three or four areas of white are prone to accidents, and should take care of their health and observe balanced life styles. This is not a Siang Mien directive to give up the good things of life, or become health fanatics. More important is that they should use their talents, but remember they are unusual in many ways because of their eyes.

TWO WHITES

THREE WHITES – ONE ABOVE IRIS

THREE WHITES – ONE BELOW IRIS

FOUR WHITES

The masters have a postscript concerning the whites of children's eyes. If the whites of young people become *bluish*, this can be taken as a sign that something is worrying or frightening them, though they may not wish to let anyone know.

Finally, *red* eyes: this is a subject that has intrigued students of Siang Mien for centuries.

Eyes that are *obviously red* indicate that a person is highly strung and likely to have a strong sex urge, often unrealised. Red eyes sometimes appear for short periods if there is too much fat in the diet.

117

Small *red dots that gather in clusters* in the whites of eyes are a reliable indication of an incipient sexual maniac.

CLUSTERS OF SMALL RED DOTS IN WHITES OF EYES

Red lines that run across, or through, the iris should be heeded as a signal that you are working too hard, and that pushing yourself to the limit will lead to over-tiredness, carelessness, and the possibility of a serious accident or illness.

RED LINES ACROSS OR THROUGH THE IRIS

Similarly, *foggy or yellowish* whites should be heeded as a sign of strain. Siang Mien warns that the wise will take a break if this discolouration appears, and adds the challenging thought that, even if you believe that the show cannot go on without you, no-one, not even an emperor, is indispensable.

CHAPTER VII
The Nose

If you ask the Chinese what 'good fortune' means the answer will be good health, good food, to be loved by the family and respected by young people when one is old. And last, but never least – money – and plenty of it.

As Chapter XIII on 'The Eight Regions' shows, it is the nose which governs wealth. Sometimes the masters of Siang Mien will talk about being 'nose to nose' with someone instead of 'face to face'. According to one Siang Mien saying: 'When your nose is itchy either you are tempted by the charms of someone, or you are tempted to spend money.'

There is no guarantee that an extremely itchy nose means you will succumb to both temptations, but in true picturesque style the Chinese say: 'When the fingers fall to scratching, the thumb follows along.' And so, if you do fall for someone's charms, it will almost certainly lead to expense.

The early masters of Siang Mien identified many different nose shapes and singled out certain features, such as nostrils, for special consideration. There is a popular Chinese saying that 'a nose with three nostrils expels too much air', attributed to those who meddle with matters that do not concern them.

And there is scant pleasure for anyone whose nose is permanently or frequently red, for an equally well-known saying reminds us that 'a red-nosed man may not be a drunkard, but he will always be called one'.

It should be borne in mind that, like eyes and mouths, noses sometimes differ according to race. For instance, Australian Aborigines have wide, flat noses and southern Chinese have flatter noses than Chinese from the north. Therefore, when practising Siang Mien make allowances for any racial features. You should estimate whether the measurements of a nose that you are observing differ from a typical nose of that race.

1. The Best Nose

The best nose for money is one that is wide at the top, moderately large, and has a rounded tip supported by fleshy sides. The nostrils should not be visible when viewed full on.

CHARLES CHAPLIN – GOOD
NOSE FOR MAKING MONEY

A *very round, fleshy tip* tells that its owner is not particularly adventurous with money, preferring to invest it safely, sometimes to the point of hoarding it. Siang Mien considers round tips lucky for their owners; such lucky people have artistic abilities and are reliably of honest intent.

A truly beautiful nose for making money not only has a round and fleshy tip, but also round, well-concealed nostrils.

2.   Arched Nose

Unless another feature of the face is very bad, an arched nose indicates luck in life. The higher the arch, the more good fortune can be expected.

WILLIAM WYLER
– ARCHED NOSE INDICATING GOOD FORTUNE

3. *Straight Nose*

Straight noses are associated with good thinking. In fact, Siang Mien shows that those with a straight nose, plus a *thin nose tip, visible nostrils and a good forehead* (smoothly rounded, wide and deep) are especially suited for top jobs and anything that requires reliability.

RAQUEL WELCH – STRAIGHT NOSE

4. *Bumpy Noses*

Two types of bumpy noses are identified by Siang Mien.

One is familiarly known as a Roman, or hook nose, although the ancient Siang Mien masters sometimes referred to it as the *shelf nose*. Having a shelf is desirable because those men and women who have this nose not only know how to look after their money, but also no-one knows how much they have.

Those who have *one or more bumps* are faced with the prospect of financial worries, especially in mid-life. However, the masters of Siang Mien urge those with bumps to put their nose to the grindstone and work hard. That, they say, is the way to overcome most hardships – financial or otherwise – though it also requires one's fair share of good fortune.

ROMAN OR HOOK NOSE   NOSE WITH TWO BUMPS

5. *Pointed Noses*

Two types of pointed noses are singled out by the Siang Mien masters. They give no name to the *downward pointing one*, but might well call it the Concorde nose to mark our supersonic times.

The Concorde nose is linked to a chilly disposition, and the more the nose points down, the colder is its owner. To this is added a Siang Mien warning: an *extremely downpointing* nose means that its owner is unreliable as a friend.

JOSEPH STALIN – DOWNWARD
POINTING NOSE

The second of the pointed noses is called the *Eagle* (aquiline) nose, which denotes cruelty.

'An eagle nose, a pockmarked face, no whiskers – with such do not associate' warn the Chinese. And a further warning comes from Siang Mien: unless those with eagle noses overcome any cruel instincts, should they live long they are doomed to a lonely old age.

KING FAISAL
– EAGLE NOSE

6. *Crooked Noses*

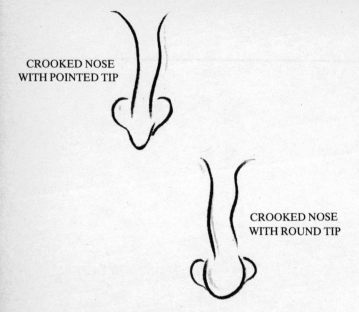

CROOKED NOSE
WITH POINTED TIP

CROOKED NOSE
WITH ROUND TIP

A crooked nose is one defect linked by Siang Mien to the Uneven Face, one of the face types described in Chapter III on 'The Face Shapes'.

The masters of Siang Mien diagnose a crooked, or lopsided, nose as one which reveals a weak and emotional character. The nose tip is important here: a *round tip* on a crooked nose shows selfishness, while a *pointed tip* is symptomatic of nastiness and an inclination to use people for self-betterment.

There is a widespread Siang Mien belief that if the nose is crooked the owner's intentions are not upright. Rather mysteriously, but no doubt based on Siang Mien experience, it is claimed that those with lopsided noses who spent their childhood in a mountainous region are less likely to be weak, emotional, or selfish than someone whose formative years took place elsewhere.

7. *Long & Short Noses*

LONG NOSE +
LARGE NOSTRILS

Long noses are indicative of stubbornness and self-pride which can, if exaggerated, lead to bad fortune and loss of friends. Some masters of Siang Mien observe that those with a *long nose and large nostrils* are mean and selfish, and should not be counted among one's close friends.

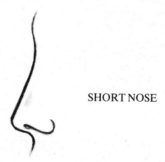

SHORT NOSE

A short nose is linked by Siang Mien to periods of financial strain and a decline of fortune around middle age.

127

8. *High & Flat Noses*

A high nose is in the Siang Mien list of desirable qualities for it indicates that this person has fewer problems over money than most.

However, a high nose that is also *long and narrow* betrays the fact that a person has difficulty saving money. Add to this a *narrow bridge* as well and the owner should be alert to a decline in fortune from forty to forty-five, but a general improvement to look forward to after that.

WOODY ALLEN – HIGH NOSE

The owners of a *high nose with a narrow, prominent bone* running down it are rarely afraid of solitude, sometimes craving it if their peace is threatened. They have to work harder than most to make a marriage work.

128

GRETA GARBO – HIGH NOSE + NARROW PROMINENT BONE

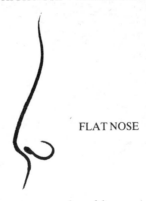

FLAT NOSE

Flat noses presage personal problems – sometimes arising from financial losses – in the mid-forties. However, most people with flat noses are not born rich, so they should economise and learn to use their money well before reaching forty.

'As a dry finger cannot take up salt,' say the masters of Siang Mien, so those with flat noses find it hard to accumulate wealth.

9. *Childish Noses*

To many, this nose with its visible nostrils is pert or cute. However, Siang Mien reveals that it is not a particularly auspicious nose as it signals moodiness, immaturity, and lack of persistence or concentration to complete a task. At times, this lack of will-power is the result of one simple fact: what they do not like they will not do.

10. *Thin Nostrils*

Not all thin nostrils are bad in the judgment of Siang Mien. Providing the *nostrils show* when viewed full face, their owner is quite adventurous and may take a major risk or two in life. Too many risks, though, are unwise, warn the masters of Siang Mien, especially for anyone with thin nostrils who enjoys gambling.

'If you believe in gambling, be prepared for the day you will have to sell your house', they tell their students.

Like eagle-shaped noses, thin nostrils are indicators of loneliness in late middle and old age. In some cases this occurs because one's children have gone away, rarely returning home. In others, friends have died or no longer call because they feel that the person with thin nostrils has changed.

NAPOLEON BONAPARTE – NOSTRILS:
THIN AND VISIBLE WHEN VIEWED FULL FACE

Armed with this knowledge, those with thin nostrils or eagle noses and still young enough, or willing, to change their ways can take steps to keep loneliness at bay by trying to understand other people better.

After all, counsel the Siang Mien masters, 'those who do not believe in others find that no-one believes in them'. And to this may be added another Chinese maxim: 'You can hardly make a friend in a year as you get older, but you can easily offend one in an hour.' So, value your friends.

11. *Plump & Thin Noses*

One's fortune is enhanced if the sides of the nose are full and fleshy.

MOTHER TERESA – PLUMP NOSE INDICATING
SPIRITUAL WEALTH

ARISTOTLE ONASSIS –
PLUMP NOSE INDICATING
WORLDLY WEALTH

Those with very narrow, or sunken, sides have to work harder than most to make a marriage succeed.

THIN NOSE +
SUNKEN SIDES

One of the problems in marriage for those with thin noses is money, the destroyer of many good relationships. For anyone for whom this problem is real, the masters of Siang Mien quote the words of the ancient Chinese: 'Those who know they have enough are rich,' and, 'it is harder to be poor without murmuring than to be rich without arrogance'.

12. *Sneezing*

It does not matter whether your sneezes are the result of a cold, hayfever, dust, a bad smell up the nose, or a moulting cat. The Chinese – but not necessarily all practitioners of Siang Mien – have one verdict: someone is talking about you!

CHAPTER VIII
The Mouth

The part of the face that can get us into deepest trouble is the mouth, and there are a number of Siang Mien sayings which show how careful we must be.

☐ Much mischief comes from opening the mouth.

☐ Once a word has left the lips the swiftest horse cannot overtake it.

☐ His mouth is honey, his heart a sword.

☐ A sharp mouth can overturn home and country.

The last was said by Confucius to his disciples, and he added: 'I wish I could do without speaking'. But if he had, the world would have been robbed of some of its most famous sayings.

As it was Confucius never conversed while eating, nor when in bed. He would not eat anything that might cause bad breath, nor food that was over-cooked, under-cooked, out of season or under-flavoured.

By looking at the shape of the mouth and its size, and by listening to the words that issue from it, Confucius and the founding fathers of Siang Mien could measure how much confidence they could place in people. There are a number of qualities to look for when studying a person's mouth.

1. *The Best Mouth*

> Your mouth is big, that's luck for you
> For happiness hangs from its corners too.

Indeed, the best mouth is, as this Siang Mien ditty shows, large. Not only should it be large, but it has to have a clear, distinct shape with corners that slope up. Each lip should be a quarter of an inch wide, and where the lips meet there should be a *straight, horizontal line*.

BARBRA STREISAND
– THE BEST MOUTH

The straighter the horizontal line, the more a person can be expected to keep promises. Siang Mien, however, advises those with this mouth: others expect you to keep promises, so do not let them down.

This perfect mouth inspires confidence in others, and its lucky owner can communicate more easily with others than can those with inferior mouths. Anyone with this mouth can expect a reasonable standard of living.

It is noticeable to anyone who practises Siang Mien that those with *big mouths* forget problems more quickly than those with small mouths. They cope better in adversity, while someone with a *small mouth* is less inclined to turn to others for help or advice, often preferring to bottle up the problem.

For those with small mouths there are some compensations. Siang Mien shows that a woman with a small mouth is more easily satisfied in love-making than one whose mouth is large. This is especially so if her fingers are also short.

A small-mouthed man, too, need not bemoan the shape of his mouth for Siang Mien reveals that he is, or could be if he tried, an inventive and appealing lover.

We have seen that Siang Mien specifies a quarter of an inch to be the ideal width for each lip. Anything wider than this is an indication of sensuality. One must remember, however, that many races and tribes characteristically have thick lips, so if one is practising Siang Mien among them these racial factors should be taken into account. It is the same with *red lips* which, Siang Mien shows, are a further indicator of sensuality. Among races with *brown or black lips*, the shape and size of the mouth become more important considerations, as does the clarity with which the outline of the mouth is distinguished from the rest of the face; a large, well defined mouth reveals passion.

2.   *Thicker Upper Lip*

A thicker upper than lower lip is a warning that the owner of this mouth should be treated cautiously, for Siang Mien reveals that this is a sign of deviousness.

Some people with this type of mouth become vegetarians for health reasons, or because they have been persuaded either by a person or by something they have seen or read, that meat is not desirable. Those who follow a mixed diet tend to enjoy meat more than most of their fellow-beings, prompting the masters of Siang Mien to refer to them affectionately as 'carnivores'.

It has been the custom in China for centuries to eat meat in bite-sized pieces, for large pork chops or thick chunks of beef are considered unsightly on the plate. The invention of chopsticks made it easier to pick up small slices of meat and, no doubt, the influence of gourmet 'carnivores' of ages past helped popularise them.

Many whose upper lips are thicker than the lower have glib tongues, and are skilful in argument.

3.   *Thicker Lower Lip*

While those with thicker upper lips can be devious, those whose lower lips are thicker may also encounter difficulties, at times, of inspiring trust. This is particularly the case if the person's *eyes are shifty, weak or watery*.

Those who are aware of their shortcomings can turn to advantage their naturally good command of speech to try entertaining others. This may be on a purely personal level at parties or private events, but many professional artists and entertainers have this type of mouth.

NOËL COWARD – THICKER LOWER LIP

4. *Receding Lower Lip*

Those whose lower lip recedes cannot depend on help from outsiders. Confucius had a suitable rule of conduct to make up for this disappointment: 'Those who are noble seek what they want in themselves, but inferior people seek it from others.'

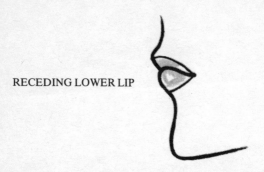

RECEDING LOWER LIP

5. *Thick Lips; Exceptionally Thin Lips*

THICK LIPS

Thick-lipped people are more likely to be sensual and emotional than those whose lips are thin. It is generally felt by those who practise Siang Mien that someone whose mouth shape resembles an *isosceles triangle* and who also has thick lips is especially susceptible to emotional fluctuations.

Exceptionally thin lips are a sign that their owners are brutal and some even enjoy humiliating others. As one would expect, they are selfish and emotionally cold. All these unattractive traits are tempered if the *tip of the nose is round*, rather than pointed.

In Siang Mien this mouth is associated with fussy eating habits and a general wariness of trying new foods.

EXCEPTIONALLY THIN LIPS

6. *The Wavy Line*

DUSTIN HOFFMAN
– MOUTH: THE WAVY LINE

If a wavy line forms where the lips meet such a person is quietly confident with words and, if called upon to address a gathering, could do very well as a public speaker. However, not even the gift of the gab is enough to ensure financial stability at all times.

Apart from this financial limitation, those with this mouth are more reliable than most, and others can feel confident in their presence.

7. *Protruding Teeth & Visible Gums*

The early masters of Siang Mien had differing opinions about the significance of protruding teeth or gums that are visible when a person smiles. Even today there are two divergent interpretations. Contradictory though they are, each contains a clear message.

Either this mouth belongs to a very generous person or to a very mean one. Siang Mien adds two thought-provoking dictums:

> To be too generous arouses the suspicion that one is buying favours and praise.

> Yet to be mean invites great unhappiness in the last years of one's life.

You will also find that many people with visible gums veer from periods of generosity to bouts of stinginess.

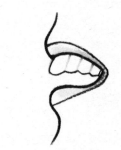

PROTRUDING TEETH

GUMS
VISIBLE WHEN
SOMEONE SMILES

8. *The Corners of the Mouth*

A mouth that *turns down* denotes over-sensitiveness, pessimism and, at the very worst, a kill-joy. If a mouth *begins to droop* and fails to recover quickly, this reveals a difficult period of new, or unresolved, problems that may take years to overcome. A *pouting* mouth betrays that its owner sulks.

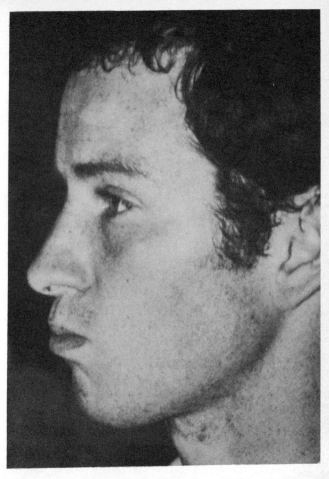

JOHN McENROE
– POUTING MOUTH

As would be expected, a mouth that *turns up* reflects happiness and optimism. Naturally, those with such a mouth have gloomy periods from time to time, but for them life is to be lived, and the more enjoyment they can get out of it, the better.

The masters of Siang Mien remind us that 'with happiness comes intelligence to the heart, and those who are happy do not notice how time goes by'. To this they add another judgment: 'The contented man, though poor, is happy. The discontented man, though rich, is sad.'

MICK JAGGER – MOUTH TURNING UP

COLONEL GADDAFI
– TINY HOLLOWS AT
CORNERS OF MOUTH

There are some mouths whose *corners recede into tiny hollows*. Siang Mien detects immediately that this person has an inferiority complex, though the untrained observer might identify this as aggression, impatience, or a supercilious attitude – all pointers of a personality problem.

147

9. *Crooked Mouth*

Whether or not you have a crooked mouth, or know someone who has, Siang Mien advises everyone to note the following Chinese story.

While hunting for a meal a tiger caught a fox.

'You can't eat me,' said the fox with a cunning, crooked smile. 'The Emperor of Heaven has appointed me king of the beasts. If you eat me you will disobey his orders. If you don't believe me, follow me. You will see that the other animals will run away at the sight of me.'

Agreeing to this the tiger let the fox go, and followed him through the forest. When all the beasts saw them coming they dashed away. Not realising that they were afraid of him, the tiger thought they were afraid of the fox.

A crooked mouth is a Siang Mien symbol of dishonesty and deceitfulness, but not all with crooked mouths have the natural cunning of a fox. If, however, someone's mouth becomes crooked through an illness, none of these factors is valid.

10. *Teeth*

The tongue is soft and remains;
The teeth are hard and fall out.

This pithy Chinese dictum says it all, but nothing can be told about character, fortune or personality from false teeth. For this one needs the real thing.

Teeth are not easy to interpret, even for the masters of Siang Mien, because personal and national eating habits vary enormously, and diet can play havoc with one's teeth. Those who nibble bones, or attack tough, sticky toffees, or grind their teeth in their sleep are liable to break or wear them down, making the task of the student of Siang Mien more difficult to identify naturally inferior teeth from damaged ones and real teeth from false. In these days of modern dentistry, one can never be sure if teeth are crowned, giving their owner a better set than the original.

Good teeth are *large*, rather than *small*. *Long* ones mean a long life.

CATHERINE DENEUVE
– GOOD TEETH

A set of *well-arranged, evenly shaped* teeth that remain *free from major defects* (such as decay and discolouration) signify that someone learns more quickly than most. This is paramount if this person also has a *fine forehead*, that is, one which is high, smoothly rounded, wide and deep.

149

The masters of Siang Mien disagree with a Western idea that *gaps* between the teeth symbolise money. On the contrary, they argue, nicely arranged teeth bring greater fortune than gappy ones.

**PRESIDENT FRANÇOIS MITTERAND
– GAPS BETWEEN TEETH**

No matter how 'good' – by Siang Mien standards – a face is, fortune is diminished if the teeth are *too variable in size*. If, for instance, the *two top front* ones are very large their owner is too stubborn. If one of these *falls out* naturally from an adult's mouth that person's fortune will not be good for a year.

VARIABLE TEETH

If both the upper and lower rows *slope inwards* be warned, say the masters of Siang Mien, of this erratic and unpredictable person.

Thick, ivory-coloured teeth generally belong to excitable people, while *thin* teeth and *very white* ones betray a fickle friend.

The last word on teeth concerns beauty. People are never totally unconcerned about their appearance, least of all the emperors and empresses of ancient China.

It is said that around 190 BC Empress Lu, reputed for her cruelty, had just condemned to a terrible death the late Emperor's favourite concubine when a message arrived from the King of the Huns proposing marriage to the Empress. Thanking him for his interest, she pointed out the reasons that prevented her from returning his affections.

'I have become short of breath, my gait is halting, and my hair and teeth are falling out.' She sent the king a gift of two imperial carriages and eight horses so that she would not have to receive his attentions again. Teeth are still a matter of concern and pride to the Chinese today, and to most of us, too.

11. The Jen-chung

This is the Siang Mien name for the groove situated between the middle of the upper lip and the base of the nose.

If it is long, its owner will live long. The early masters of Siang Mien had a theory that an inch represented 100 years, and today some followers of Siang Mien maintain that as a rule of thumb, so to speak, the Jen-chung indicates whether one will become a centenarian. That one's lifespan is in direct ratio to the length of the Jen-chung is more uncertain.

In recent times, the theory has developed that from the Jen-chung can be told certain Siang Mien facts about happiness and family relationships.

Siang Mien reveals that those with this Jen-chung had periods of conflict or doubt in an unsettled childhood which still affect them throughout their adult life.

This Jen-chung has two parallel lines, signs of a long life and indicators of a firm and determined character, capable of inspiring a sound family tradition.

This Jen-chung shows a tendency to find life more difficult and problematic with the passing years. Early promise proves difficult to fulfil, and some hopes are never realised.

CHAPTER IX
The Ear

In the south-west of China in the year 220 lived a man called Liu Pei. At this time the country was divided into warring states to the north and south of the great Yangtze river. Claiming descent from the royal family of Han, Liu Pei founded a new dynasty, and prepared his followers for war.

Liu Pei has fascinated students of Siang Mien for centuries for he was reputed to have huge ears like an elephant's, ears that reached to his shoulders.

No-one knows whether or not this was an exaggeration, but ideally, say the Siang Mien masters, the ears should be large and rather soft.

The first books written about Siang Mien contained drawings not only of people with ears stretching to the shoulders, but to the ground. Almost all these books were destroyed in China's turbulent past when palaces and their libraries of precious books were frequently sacked and burnt, but writers of the Ming dynasty referred to these records of ideal ears of extreme length.

The ears govern the period from a person's birth to the age of fourteen. Siang Mien cannot be practised with reliability on the face – still changing and developing – of anyone under fourteen, so ears are the most positive source of information for that age. Successive generations of masters and students of Siang Mien have put together some important particulars about the ear, including the relation of the ear lobe to one's sex drive.

1. *Size & Position*

In modern times the Maasai of Kenya continue the custom of stretching their ears by attaching metal weights, glass beads or wooden discs to their lobes, some of which grow to four inches long.

The ears now considered by Siang Mien as most auspicious are still *large* ones. However, it is no advantage to have large ears that are disproportionate to the size of the face. *Large ears on a small face* betray a lack of substance and a shallow character. Yet, these are lucky people whom others like and readily help. Despite the assistance and opportunities that come their way, those with large ears and small faces find it difficult to grasp and hold on to power.

POPE JOHN PAUL II – WELL PROPORTIONED LARGE EARS

Small ears inform Siang Mien observers that these are men and women who work hard, unable as they are to rely on support from others. Though ambitious, a lack of confidence can cause a gap between what they want and what they can achieve.

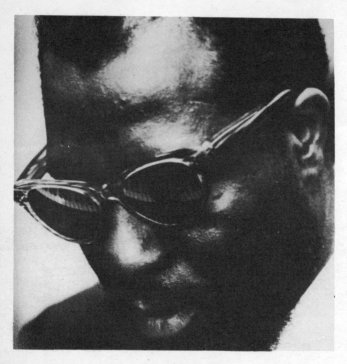

THELONIUS MONK
– SMALL EARS

The simplest way of telling whether people's ears are well positioned is to draw two imaginary, parallel lines through the eyebrows and the tip of the nose. For good fortune the ear should lie entirely between the two lines, but it will surprise most people to see that many ears are too high or too low.

The chances of being famous before thirty are increased if the ears *extend above the line of the eyebrows*, but this is no guarantee that good fortune or wealth will last for ever. Those who hope for fame and success would be advised to bear in mind what Confucius had to say about this: 'Those who are wise are not distressed that people do not know them; they are distressed at their own lack of ability.'

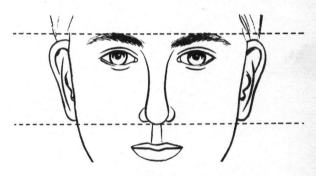

EARS SHOULD BE BETWEEN
THE TWO LINES

Those with *low-placed* ears are likely to achieve most late in life. Deng Xiaopeng's photo on p. 41 provides a splendid example. How much will be achieved can be told from the lower part of the face, particularly the chin (see Chapter XI on 'The Chin').

2. *Shape*

Ears should be *flat*, an indication of good fortune and stable family relationships. There is a Chinese belief that if an ear is so flat that a finger cannot fit anywhere behind it this person will live beyond eighty.

Many people have *protruding* ears. However slightly ears protrude, they indicate that their owners need to draw on inner reserves of strength and ability to get on in life.

**PRINCE CHARLES,
MAHATMA GANDHI, LAUREL AND HARDY
ALL HAVE PROTRUDING EARS**

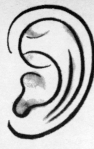 

ROUND EAR   SQUARISH EAR

Besides being flat, the best ears are also *round*, declare the masters of Siang Mien. Round ears denote wealth and kindness, while ears which are *squarish* – also considered desirable by Siang Mien – contribute to a person's wealth and cleverness.

LONG EARS

Those with *long* ears instinctively help only those who deserve help, and uncannily sense when someone is trying to take advantage of them.

POINTED EAR

LOUIS ARMSTRONG
– THICK EARS

Pointed tips – upper or lower, but especially upper ones – inform the Siang Mien observer that these people are more stubborn and generally more efficient and conscientious in what they do than most.

Thick ears are more desirable than *thin* ears: thick ones contribute to good fortune, but thin ones are associated with physical weakness and periods of indifferent health.

161

An ear that is *markedly wider at the top* than the lower half can tell a Siang Mien student that its owner excels in one particular subject.

**BUSTER KEATON – EARS MARKEDLY
WIDER AT THE TOP**

3. *Outer & Inner Circles*

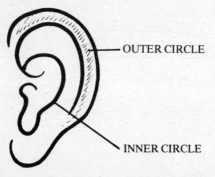

OUTER CIRCLE

INNER CIRCLE

Siang Mien divides the ear into visible outer and inner circles. Those who are blessed with a large and well shaped ear (round, smooth, soft, thick) plus well defined inner and outer circles can make a success of most things they set their hearts on.

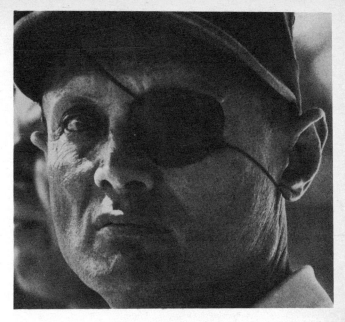

GENERAL MOSHE DAYAN
– EAR WITH PROMINENT
INNER CIRCLE

Those whose inner circle is more prominent than the
outer have stamina, and will see through any project,
scheme, or task they set their minds to.

If the ear is comparatively large, but the inner circle is not
well defined (or is lower than the outer circle, or receding)
this person should not expect to advance very high up the
executive ladder unless the forehead is so good (round,
smooth, high, wide and deep) that it compensates for the
ear.

If the inner or outer circle, or both, sticks out to form a
sharp corner or bend on its perimeter, an unhappy event
that took place between the ages of three and four has left
its mark: this person takes things for granted, and this lack
of gratitude can severely harm relationships.

4. *Lobes*

The lobes tell the Siang Mien observer something about a person's love life.

Small lobes are tell-tale signs that insecure relationships with parents or elders have caused emotional blocks or hang-ups that affect the enjoyment of sex.

SMALL LOBE + ROUND,
WIDE INNER CIRCLE

The problem is lessened if the inner circle of the ear (discussed in the previous section of this chapter) is round and wide. In fact, this combination of a *small lobe with a round and wide inner circle* tells the Siang Mien observer that here indeed is someone with an exceedingly strong sex urge.

Add to this a round outer ear, and the owner is not only interested in sex, but liable to prove much too lusty for all but those having the same type of ear!

Tiny lobes on round ears allow Siang Mien observers to identify a fairly stubborn person fond of material comforts.

The best lobes are *large and thick*, for nice fleshy lower ears are a sign of fortune and ability to accumulate more wealth than average. Even those who are unable to save money because of their poorly shaped nose (see Chapter VII on 'The Nose') can reap some benefit from having good ear lobes. For, according to Siang Mien, having good lobes not only brings good fortune, but is the key to having links with people who can help.

It is like, say the Siang Mien masters, being the rich man who asks a favour and is invited in, made to feel welcome, and supplied with more than he requested before being sent happily on his way. On the other hand, if a poor or unlucky man asks the same, he is scorned and treated like a thief.

ALFRED HITCHCOCK
– THE BEST LOBE

If the lobe *protrudes and slants towards the mouth*, this indicates that fortune will improve late in life.

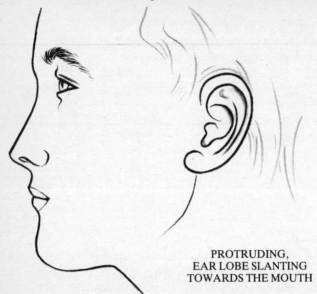

PROTRUDING,
EAR LOBE SLANTING
TOWARDS THE MOUTH

Immediately above the lobe, the inner circle dips down to form a *gap*. The more generous a person is, the wider the gap. It should comfortably accommodate your forefinger if you have a free and easy attitude to giving. Anything tighter shows a more penny-pinching attitude.

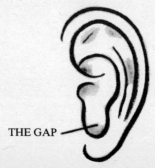

THE GAP

166

Behind the gap is the *ear hole*. A *deep* one typifies someone with a probing mind while a *small, shallow* one belongs to those who are not especially interested in other people.

A *wide* ear hole is associated with argumentative people who do not easily believe what others tell them. The masters of Siang Mien quote Confucius to these people: 'If you are disliked at forty, so you will be to the end.' A fair warning, but one which they are likely to disregard.

HAIRY EAR

Some people are naturally more hairy than others. If there is a *heavy growth of hair* in the ear that is disproportionate to the rest of the body, this communicates to the Siang Mien onlooker that these people waste their talent and dissipate their energies.

The masters of Siang Mien conclude their observations of the ear by linking it to the eyes and heart.

'When the ear will not listen the heart escapes sorrow. But when you have heard, you must heed; when you have seen, you must judge in your heart.'

So much depends upon the eyes and the ears of the world.

CHAPTER X
Cheeks & Cheekbones

According to popular opinion in the West, the most attractive cheekbones are high ones, and in particular *high cheekbones* are thought to enhance a woman's beauty.

This is not the Siang Mien concept of good cheekbones. For one thing, say the masters of Siang Mien without attempting to appeal to human vanity, 'those with bones sticking out under the eyes' have hollow, or even sunken, cheeks. They look lean and hungry and they prematurely age, so that by the time they are forty, or thirty-five in some cases, they look older than they are, whilst those with plump cheeks often look years younger than their true age.

The Siang Mien ideal of a beautiful cheek and cheekbones is a slightly *rounded* look in which skin and bone are well balanced. The masters of Siang Mien turn to China's most famous novel to illustrate their point.

The Dream of the Red Chamber was written in the eighteenth century, and to weave his story of love and fiendish family intrigues, the author uses no less than 421 characters – 232 males and 189 females. In one scene a young girl describes her first impressions of a handsome man: 'His clothes were shabby, yet he was powerfully built with an open face, firm lips, eyebrows like scimitars, eyes like stars, a straight nose, and rounded cheeks.'

Rounded cheeks are prized because they reveal that their owner has more command of power than someone with

CHAIRMAN MAO
TSETUNG AND QUEEN
VICTORIA HAD ONE
THING IN COMMON:
PLUMP, ROUNDED
CHEEKS

high cheekbones or *lean, low, or flat* cheeks. People will think twice, maybe more than twice, before trying to take advantage of those with round cheeks.

The masters of Siang Mien have yet more good words for rounded cheeks. They liken them to peaches: round, smooth and pink. And they quote two lines from a poem about a sailor's wife written in the eighth century by one of China's greatest poets, Li Po:

Pity me now, when I was fifteen
My face was as pink as a peach's skin.

169

Today, doting grandmothers in China can be seen cuddling their small grandchildren and playfully nibbling their bright pink cheeks, which they call 'peach cheeks'. Biting peaches also constituted a large part of the day's work for Monkey, a favourite Chinese mythological character who, like the Chinese themselves, believes that peaches contain the secret of immortality.

'It is better to take one bite of peach than to eat a basketful of apricots' is the Chinese way of saying that a little of the best is more desirable than a lot of something inferior.

MUHAMMAD ALI – GLISTENING,
ROUNDED CHEEKS

Siang Mien provides additional information for those with *dark skins* and for whom pink cheeks might well be irrelevant and unimportant. Rounded cheeks are still the best, but they are perfect if the skin on the cheekbones *glistens*. As with pink cheeks, people will not readily try to get the better of those with rounded cheekbones and dark, glistening skin.

GENERAL ALEXANDER HAIG HAS
THE THREE IMPORTANT INGREDIENTS
OF A SUCCESSFUL SOLDIER'S FACE

So far, all the praise from the masters of Siang Mien has been for rounded cheeks. There is, however, some compensation for those with prominent cheekbones.

If the *cheekbones are the widest part of the face* this means that someone is good at tackling matters that need attention, and the job will be done, even if it takes a long time. Those with wide, prominent cheekbones do not have a large number of close friends, in part because others are jealous of them, and because others cannot resist criticising any decision or action that those with prominent cheekbones take.

As in all Siang Mien teaching one particular feature should not be considered in isolation. This is especially important with high cheekbones.

For instance, Siang Mien nominates three important ingredients that a man hoping for a successful career in the armed forces should possess: *prominent cheekbones, sunken cheeks and a strong jaw*.

171

Yet, *prominent cheekbones combined with a very pointed chin* indicate someone who lacks the affection and faithfulness needed to be a true friend.

Again, *sharply defined, high cheekbones that slant upwards* belong to those who see themselves as the dominant figure at home. At worst, they will make use of friends, and sometimes their families, to achieve their goals.

Another important Siang Mien observation concerns those who have both *high cheekbones and severely sunken cheeks*. They can expect their fortunes to take a tumble during the period from thirty to fifty. If, say the masters of Siang Mien, the severely sunken cheeks are caused by ill-health, seek the type of medicine or treatment for which the body has an affinity. If the sunken cheeks are caused by dieting and vanity, then, say the masters of Siang Mien, no medicine can cure a vulgar or foolish person.

PROMINENT CHEEKBONES
+ VERY POINTED CHIN

Low, flat cheekbones deserve a separate comment. The masters of Siang Mien observe that this type of cheekbone conveys acquiescence and an inclination to side-step a challenge or conflict. *Very flat* cheekbones betray humility and cowardice.

The masters of Siang Mien urge these people to think about the Chinese suggestion that 'wise people make their own decisions, while foolish ones follow public opinion'. And to this they add the tale that is told to a frightened child.

In the jungle the tiger and the leopard are afraid to meet the unicorn, and even the mighty dragon is scared of something: the centipede. Just as some people fear moths, spiders or little lizards, so the dragon has his phobia, too.

All of us – even the most powerful – one day meet someone of whom we are afraid.

LOW, FLAT CHEEKBONES

**SUNKEN AREAS MARKED 'X'
= SOMEONE DISAPPOINTED IN
LOVE, ESPECIALLY IN MARITAL
RELATIONSHIPS**

LINE RUNNING FROM INNER EYE ACROSS CHEEKBONE

The masters of Siang Mien comment on *a line* that runs from the inner tip of the eye (by the nose) across the cheekbone. This is hardly auspicious, for it indicates one or more of the following: periods of disharmony at home during the period from thirty to fifty years (of age, not marriage); difficulty retaining money; being used by others to further their ambitions or desires.

However, Siang Mien urges those who have this line not to suspect that everyone they know or meet is out to get the better of them. On the contrary, say the Siang Mien masters, to know is to be forewarned, and their advice is simply:

'Let your practice keep step with your knowledge.'

CHAPTER XI
The Chin

When the first emperor of China died he was buried in an enormous underground chamber constructed by more than 700,000 labourers. Artisans fixed automatic crossbows so that any grave-robbers who broke in would be slain. The emperor's childless concubines were buried with him, and to prevent those who were closely acquainted with the contents of the tomb from revealing what they knew they, too, were buried.

As if this were not enough, an army of more than 7,000 life-size, pottery figures of armoured soldiers, crossbowmen, spearmen, charioteers, horsemen and their horses and chariots were buried in military formation in another chamber. This army was to protect the emperor on his journey to the next world.

The emperor, Ch'in Shi Huangti, is best known outside China as the builder of the Great Wall of China. In 1974, nearly 2,200 years after his death, the pit containing the pottery army figures was discovered and excavated.

No two faces of the pottery men are identical, for they were modelled on individual soldiers from throughout the Ch'in empire. As one would expect of a nation who discovered Siang Mien, each soldier has a strong, virile face, most evident in the powerful nose and strong chin.

It is to the chin that one looks in order to discover what kind of old age a person will have, for the chin holds the secret of the years from fifty-one until the angels sing.

PRESIDENT JOHN F. KENNEDY AND HIS WIFE, JACQUELINE
– HERS IS THE MORE POWERFUL CHIN

The most powerful chins are those which *stick out*. The
weakest are those which *recede*.

A good chin is a *smoothly curving, round* one which
forms part of a smooth, strong jaw. Together they symbolise a nice, comfortable old age.

There is nothing inferior about a *square* chin either.
Look at Robert Redford's on p. 54. It, too, represents
power plus an additional qualification of leadership skills:
those with square chins are better suited to be leaders than
subordinates.

Those with *round or square* chins are most likely to live
longest. Anyone with a *wide jaw* can also look forward to a
good lifespan, providing the chin is good.

RECEDING CHIN

Siang Mien has additional observations about *receding* chins. These people are less ambitious than most; they do not stretch themselves to their mental or physical limits. Siang Mien also reveals that, though some people with receding chins coast along through life and enjoy a reasonably good middle age, there is a likelihood of a dramatic change of fortune in later life which will require a strong will to overcome problems affecting health and good fortune.

The chin also provides a useful yardstick for employers. Look here, say the masters of Siang Mien, if you are thinking of going into business with someone. A *full, rounded* chin that is smooth and free from bumps intimates that here is a person who would be a helpful business partner.

INDENTS BELOW
CORNERS OF MOUTH

However, any *small indents* immediately below the corners of the mouth reveal that this person is slow to delegate responsibility and power, and is therefore likely to clash with employees. But – there is an exception. If such a person has a *square* chin, then this chin can overrule most problems arising over employees.

Both *round and square* chins come to the rescue of someone with an inferior Career Region (the area of the forehead described in Chapter XIII on 'The Eight Regions'). Although Siang Mien advises those with an indented or flat forehead against employing others or going into business on their own, a good, strong chin can help overcome these problems.

FLESHY, ALMOST THREE-DIMENSIONAL, CIRCULAR AREA ON CHIN

A *fleshy, almost three-dimensional, circular* area in the centre of the chin reveals that a person's love life is not very smooth. This disturbance may stem from an earlier marriage or a meaningful friendship that floundered.

This same circular area also indicates a powerful sex urge. Siang Mien shows that the more three-dimensional the circle is, the more sexually demanding is its owner.

A surprisingly large number of people have a *cleft* in the chin. Its main significance is that its owner enjoys praise, some even craving the spotlight. Many people with this chin marry more than once.

HUMPHREY BOGART
– CLEFT IN CHIN

Beards

Not many Chinese can grow a proper beard, having to be satisfied with thin wisps of hair. It is quite usual for Siang Mien masters to tell their students an old Chinese adage:

It is hard to touch the reflection of flowers in a mirror or the moon in a stream;
But it is even harder to have all these three – good sons, old age, and a long beard.

The early masters of Siang Mien deplored the efforts of men to grow beards, believing that a truly civilised man should be hairless and smooth skinned.

In recent times, the masters of Siang Mien have perceived that men grow beards for one or more of the following reasons: to hide an inferior chin or ugly jaw; to conceal a double chin which, they say, is a sign of over-eating and lassitude and generally goes with a fat belly; to affect intellectual inclinations or assume primitive appearances (Westerners might prefer to call these 'artistic' appearances); to conceal pimples, blemishes and warts; laziness; to keep warm.

This last explanation for growing a beard has gained support since the Chinese themselves climbed Mount Everest, for the masters of Siang Mien have noticed that most mountaineers grow beards for warmth. The Chinese call the mighty mountain which they share with Nepal, Mount Qomolangma.

Siang Mien reveals that men who grow *thick* beards work hard to achieve their ambitions and goals. Able to turn their minds to a number of subjects, many have problems deciding in which field their true talents lie. As a result of searching – as often mentally and emotionally as physically – for an answer, they dissipate their energies, sometimes wasting talent, too.

Men who can only grow *sparse* beards do not know their true worth. Unwilling to push their talents to the limit – often because they fear failure – many could achieve more in life by taking some chances instead of exercising caution.

A *bald patch* (or patches) in the beard tells the world that this man might well have been suited to living in a bygone age, one which would have appealed more to his values and aspirations.

FIDEL CASTRO
– THICK BEARD

CHÉ GUEVARA
– SPARSE BEARD

CHAPTER XII
Moles

There are countless places on the face where moles can be found, but Siang Mien reveals that those described below are the most significant.

A. Mentally mature early.
B. An illness or disease is struggling to take hold; if it wins, it could surface at around forty-one.
C. As with B a health problem is likely. If the illness or disease wins, it would appear in the mid-forties.
D. Beware of a loss of money at forty-eight. This is least likely to be embarrassing if the tip of the nose is round.
E. This mole reveals three features:
    a) a warning against accidents in the water, especially in the sea.
    b) if a woman, difficulty with the birth of her baby.
    c) if a man, at around fifty-one problems with a colleague, or a superior, at work.
F. A mole anywhere on the lips or close to the corners of the top lip reveals a general enjoyment of food, but digestive problems are likely after forty. Siang Mien also warns against accidents at sea.
G. Quick to make decisions.
H. Serious thinker at an early age.
I. Rather aggressive and stern, but ability to supervise others.
J. A mole on the chin (except mid-chin) or moles scattered around the chin signify a lonely old age.

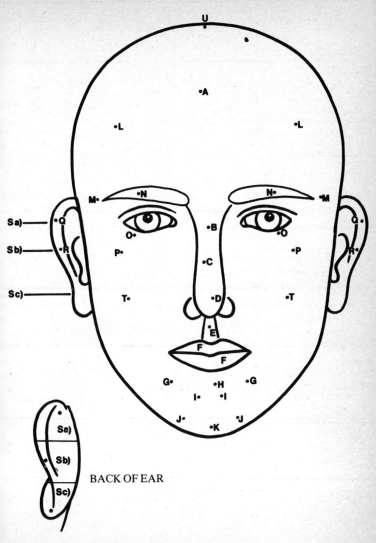

BACK OF EAR

K. One parent may have died or become emotionally detached while you were young.
L. Would be a good wife or husband.

M. A mole (or moles) between the end of the eyebrows and the hairline denotes a rather pensive person, even melancholic at times, who may not even be happy despite a successful career or what others might enviously call a 'successful lifestyle'.

N. A mole (or moles) on any part of the eyebrow belong to those who are comparatively well off; accident prone between thirty-one and thirty-four.

O. Moles here have different meanings for men and women:
   a) a woman: if the mole is on the left, she outlives her husband. If the mole is on the right, her children have some health problems.
   b) a man: if the mole is on the right, he outlives his wife. If the mole is on the left, his children have some health problems.

P. This is the 'beauty-spot' position near the cheekbone. Two moles (one on each 'beauty-spot' position) increase a person's power. A single mole reduces personal power.

Q. This person is more gifted than average.

R. There are obstacles to accomplishing important tasks. If the middle of the outer circle (edge) of the ear is pointed, this person is very ambitious.

S. This mole (or moles) is at the back of the ear:
   a) upper ear = problem with parents.
   b) middle ear = others try to benefit from your hard work or ideas.
   c) lower ear = adverse effect on wealth.

T. This mole is right in the middle of the cheek. A mole on *one* cheek means these people die in a place far from their birthplace. A mole on *each* cheek signifies a happy old age (except for those whose chins are poor: see Chapter XI on 'The Chin').

U. This is the luckiest mole of all. In fact, it is the luckiest part of the head, but unless you are bald on top, finding out whether you have the lucky spot will be tricky. This mole means that its lucky owner can change bad to good.

These are the twenty-one most significant moles. The masters of Siang Mien know that there are also a number of moles which reveal important information about people. However, because of the intimate parts of the body involved, you may not have occasion to discover whether many people have these moles or not.

☐ On the kneecap = can keep money.
☐ In the middle of the groin = over-sexed.
☐ Very centre of the armpit = money-maker.
☐ Immediately below the navel, half an inch to either side = kind; original ideas.
☐ Between the buttocks = artistic; eager to learn.

CHAIRMAN MAO TSETUNG'S
FAMOUS MOLE

CHAPTER XIII
The Eight Regions

After the Three Zones of the face (see Chapter IV), Siang Mien further divides the three areas into Eight Regions: eight is considered by those who practise Siang Mien (and also by Taoists) as a lucky number.

The Eight Regions are:

1. Life Region

2. Pulse Points

3. Career Region

4. Wealth Region

5. Friendship Region

6. Parental Region

7. Health and Energy Region

8. Love Region

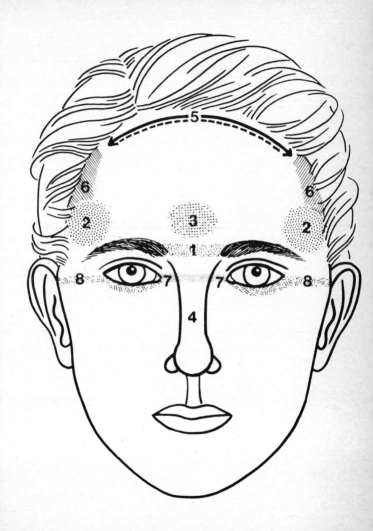

1. *Life Region*

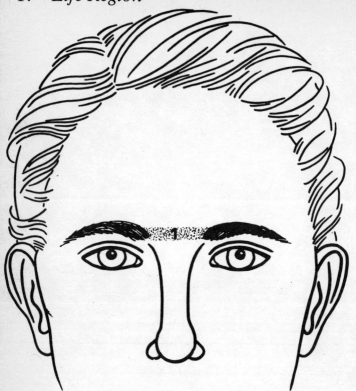

This is the area between the eyebrows. As the most important region of the face, it governs everything about us. If it turns *grey suddenly*, life is in danger.

Most Chinese can talk about life and death without fear; they do not suffer the inhibitions which make many people regard death as a taboo subject. 'The world's affairs are but a dream in spring' they say. 'Look upon death as a going home.'

The masters of Siang Mien believe that a good life is one which is stable, advancing smoothly without too many highs and lows in health, luck, or any aspect of personal behaviour. This does not mean that life has to be dull. Confucius called this steady path of good fortune the Golden Medium, and urged all to seek it.

Those whose Life Region is *wide, smooth and flat* are most likely to attain the Golden Medium. The region should be one and a half to two fingers wide, more if the face is wide. The wider the Life Region, the more tolerant, forgiving and generous a person is. Smoothness and flatness also contribute to wealth.

Conversely, someone with a narrow, bumpy Life Region tends to bear grudges, and is rarely noted for generosity.

Anyone with a *poor forehead* – bumpy, flat, very narrow, or pointed – is likely to have had a difficult childhood, but the effects of this will be mitigated for those who have a good Life Region that is smooth, flat and wide.

A Life Region that is *narrow and slopes abruptly towards the nose* indicates an uneven ride with lots of ups and downs, and little likelihood of accumulating a great fortune.

According to Siang Mien, the eyebrows and the Life Region together reveal:

(i) A Life Region that *slopes abruptly down towards the nose coupled with a prominent area immediately above the eyebrows* spotlights a twenty-fifth birthday that heralds a hard-working period which could be a turning point with every chance of a much smoother life to follow.

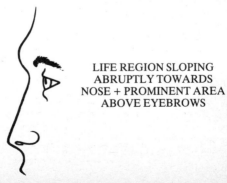

LIFE REGION SLOPING
ABRUPTLY TOWARDS
NOSE + PROMINENT AREA
ABOVE EYEBROWS

HAIR GROWING BETWEEN EYEBROWS

(ii) *Hair* growing in this region (sometimes as an extension of the eyebrows, but not necessarily) is a trait of ungenerous and unforgiving types, so it is best not to tread on the toes of those who have this feature.

(iii) The *worry crease*: a line, or series of lines or grooves that run down the Life Region between the eyebrows symbolises one or more of the following: people who work hard, who do not get much parental assistance or encouragement with their careers, who left home early, or left home to travel abroad.

RUPERT MURDOCH
– WORRY CREASE

PRESIDENT JIMMY CARTER
– WORRY CREASE

2.   *Pulse Points*

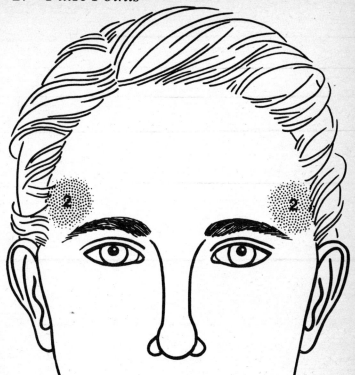

The two Pulse Points tell whether people have easy lives, or not.

Good Pulse Points are *full, rounded and hairless*. Less desirable are those which *slope away, or are hairy, or both*. Hair growing at these points signifies that someone has to work relatively hard throughout life, expending a lot of energy, some of it unnecessarily. This obdurate determination to drive oneself to achieve a goal is described by the Chinese with the saying: 'If you continually grind a bar of iron, you can make a needle of it'.

Siang Mien shows that it is advisable, when studying people's foreheads, to consider the Pulse Points with care.

Some people may have one or more of the qualities which constitute a good forehead – wide, deep, rounded, smooth – yet have poor Pulse Points. They may appear to be happy, but flawed Pulse Points signal many unsolved problems, some arising in childhood. The Chinese describe such people as 'those who laugh on the outside and cry on the inside'.

On a *narrow forehead*, the Pulse Points and the Parental Region (the sixth region described in this chapter) are close together. Siang Mien associates this with emotional ups and downs leading, in some cases, to periods of emotional imbalance.

3. Career Region

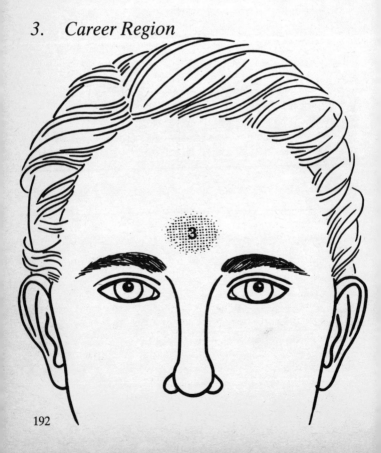

This is a vital area and third in importance of the Eight Regions.

Situated above the Life Region in the centre, it was used by the original masters of Siang Mien to estimate how far a man would advance up the imperial ladder of power, even enabling them to predict whether he would rise to a top position at the emperor's court. Now, students of Siang Mien look to this area as a guide to careers in general.

A good Career Region has a *smooth and rounded bone structure*. Not only is this indicative of a successful career, but it shows that someone so endowed can count on the support of bosses and subordinates, as well as outsiders.

YEHUDI MENUHIN
– GOOD CAREER REGION

Those with *indented, angular, or bumpy* Career Regions are not to be trusted, said the founding fathers of Siang Mien. While this may be too severe a judgment today, it can be said that although those with a poor Career Region are not necessarily more dishonest than anyone else, many have themselves learnt to be wary of others.

Those whose Career Regions are imperfect are therefore keen to make the most of every opportunity, and many believe in the Chinese proverb that 'learning which does not advance each day will daily decrease'. Success, if it comes at all, is unlikely before thirty.

Siang Mien adds a cautionary note: there is a considerable gap between ambition and achievement for many with poor Career Regions; to be forewarned lessens disappointments.

An *especially indented or flat* Career Region is a sign that one should not go into business on one's own account or be an employer, for the chances of surviving more than five years are slim. By then it may be too late to find a good job.

The Career Region & the Chin

However, there is an important Siang Mien link between the Career Region and the chin as an indicator of business skills. A *good chin* that is full, smooth and rounded can counteract the disadvantages of an indented or flat Career Region, so there is no reason why anyone with such a chin should not enter a business partnership.

It is also worth considering the shape of the chin when choosing a business partner; a good chin confirms that its owner will be a helpful associate.

A *strong, square chin* is also able to offset the weaknesses associated with an inferior Career Region, but in either case – a square chin or a round one – even the business flair attributed to the chin is weakened if there are small indents just below the mouth tips on each side of the mouth.

Over the centuries, the Siang Mien masters have noticed that those whose Career Region is good can afford to make mistakes in business. In fact, they are able to recoup losses.

4. *Wealth Region*

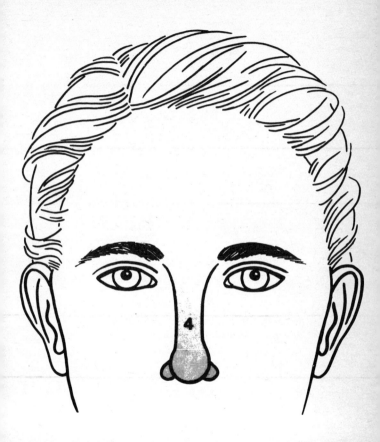

The nose is the only *organ* of the face which is one of the Eight Regions. All the rest are *areas* of the face. The nose governs wealth, so there is truth in the saying that some people have a nose for money.

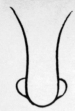

A GOOD NOSE FOR MAKING MONEY

The masters of Siang Mien have devised a picturesque concept for the nose: if it is *wide across the top* like a money box, plenty of money will fall in. A *big* nose can hold more money, but if the *nostrils show* when viewed full face, the money falls out of the bottom. *Small* noses, like small money boxes, cannot hold much money.

The ideal nose is *straight and without bumps*, and it has a *round, plump tip* which is supported by *fleshy, concealed nostrils*.

This early concept was added to later: if the *lower ridge* of the nose is *bumpy or marred by moles, lines or blotches*, the money supply is threatened by inefficient paymasters or bad debtors.

Siang Mien adds an afterthought about the *chin*, linking it with the nose in matters of wealth. A round or square, slightly protruding chin permits you to retain, or perhaps add to, a fortune in later years. If it recedes it is advisable to entrust your fortune – however large or modest – to the care of a trustworthy person or institution, and not to attempt financial decisions on your own behalf.

Siang Mien shows that money and property – in other words, material wealth – are important components of 'good fortune'. The following ancient proverb therefore appeals to most Chinese:

> If you are poor, though you dwell in the busy market-place, no-one will enquire about you. If you are rich, though you live in the heart of the mountains, you will have distant relatives.

There is more to the nose than being the Wealth Region, as you will see in Chapter VII, which features different types of noses.

5. Friendship Region

'New clothes and old friends are the best', say many who practise Siang Mien. By looking at the Friendship Region they can tell who is likely to make friends easily.

The Friendship Region is where the top of the face meets the hairline. This is a curious region which also reveals certain aspects about travel.

Siang Mien considers a good hairline one which is *high and sweeps smoothly* from one side of the face to the other. The *two corners*, which should be *wide*, should also be *hairless*.

Those with good Friendship Regions not only make friends readily, but find that their friends are able and willing to help them when required. These are indeed fortunate people, for they can also count on assistance from their family.

PRINCESS MARGARET
– GOOD FRIENDSHIP REGION

Those, however, who have *hair growing on the corner* areas of the Friendship Region, cannot depend on help from their friends who, in most instances, are not only less capable than they are themselves, but also poorer.

'V' HAIRLINE

Based on observing foreign visitors to China and on the observations of Chinese emissaries who journeyed abroad, some Siang Mien masters during the Ming dynasty noted that a characteristic of some who travelled far or frequently was a type of hairline that some would today describe as the 'widow's peak'; that is, a hairline which dips in the middle of the forehead to form a 'V', and rises above each corner to form a rounded or pointed peak.

They went on to add that many of these people form friendships easily, but pay to keep them. Pleasant though these friendships may be, few will last a lifetime.

'Gold is plentiful in the world but white-haired friends are few' is one Chinese saying. 'When you have tea and wine you have many friends' is another Chinese belief with which those with V-hairlines are more likely to agree.

Individuals with *low hairlines, narrow foreheads and hairy corners* work harder than most, with little of the financial rewards they hope for; this is particularly so before thirty. These features are also warnings that ill health is likely to be a family problem.

LOW HAIRLINE, NARROW FOREHEAD, HAIRY CORNERS

6. *Parental Region*

Immediately below the corner areas of the Friendship Region (the fifth Region) is the Parental Region. Its importance should not be underrated. The masters of Siang Mien and the sage Confucius believed – as indeed do nearly all Chinese today – that children should honour their parents.

The founding fathers of Siang Mien perceived that those whose Parental Region is *nicely rounded and curved* inherit more character traits from their parents than those whose Parental Region *slopes back* from the face.

EVA PERON – PARENTAL
REGION SLOPING
BACK FROM FACE

QUEEN ELIZABETH II – THREE
GOOD REGIONS: PARENTAL,
FRIENDSHIP, PULSE POINTS

This is likely to be bad news to those who consider their parents to be particularly awful. But, said the ancient Siang Mien masters, there are unlimited opportunities for self-improvement, and no-one should blame parents for bad fortune.

They also quoted a number of instructions concerning filial piety, many of which would upset the twentieth century man and woman, but some are worth considering.

'Before fathers and mothers, uncles and aunts, itch as you may but you dare not scratch.'

Outrageous? Later masters of Siang Mien had a saying which may be more acceptable today.

'If you wish for dutiful children first show filial piety to your own parents.'

Though countless venerable sages of ancient China spoke about filial piety and inheriting wisdom, it was more the concern of the Siang Mien masters that parents should be able to assist their children materially, as well as spiritually.

So, their observations led to the evolution of the theory that those whose *Parental Region is good, but whose Pulse Points* (the second Region) *and Friendship Region* (the fifth Region) *are inferior* would, alas, be in no position to be assisted financially.

Conversely, they remarked that those who have all *three regions nicely smooth and rounded* would be better off because their parents would be able to introduce them to influential people.

While modern students of Siang Mien consider the links between family influence and wealth and the three regions of the forehead less applicable today, they do not deny another connection that the founding fathers of Siang Mien made between these three regions and intelligence: that those fortunate to have *three nicely smooth and rounded regions* have inherited keen intelligence from the family.

And so, without realising it, the earliest practitioners of Siang Mien were identifying, through observing faces, the influence of genes long before the study of genetics became scientific.

As with the Friendship Region, the early Siang Mien masters were preoccupied with *hair covering* the Parental Region, attributing any hairiness here as a sign of having a parent who has mistresses or lovers, or who remarries.

They linked this same marital and sexual pattern of behaviour in one's parents to anyone whose *forehead is higher on one side* than the other, and to those whose Parental, Friendship, and Pulse Points *all slope* markedly away from the face.

7. Health & Energy Region

This is the area between the eyes, including the bridge of the nose. It is immediately below the first Region – the Life Region.

A *wide, flat* region is a sign of good health. A *narrow* one reveals health troubles, including a lot of minor problems; in some cases there is a low resistance to disease, so care should be taken when travelling in countries where diseases are endemic.

In the fourth century AD, Chinese alchemists, some of whom practised Siang Mien, devised a set of rules which,

1,600 years later, still ring true. Simple though the instructions sound, they are also pure commonsense, a commodity that even the best of us sometimes ignore. Here are some examples:

☐ Put on extra clothes before feeling cold.

☐ Eat before feeling hungry.

☐ Never eat to capacity.

☐ Eat moderately before going to sleep.

They also had this to say to those who had problems rising early in the morning:

☐ To get up early for three mornings is equal to one day in time.

Lines across the Health and Energy Region are quite common, but they have a variety of causes and meanings.

Some lines represent past problems, even catastrophes, that occurred in childhood. Others forewarn of something unpleasant at around forty-one, though this may be nothing more serious than a short illness of minor consequence, however unpleasant it may be at the time. Or, lines running through this region can be signs that an operation is recommended around the age of forty.

ACUTE SLOPE BETWEEN LIFE REGION AND HEALTH &
ENERGY REGION

More likely to be of lasting significance than any lines, said the early practitioners of Siang Mien, is an *acute slope* between the Life Region (the first Region situated between the eyebrows) and the Health and Energy Region. This indicates that minor health problems will occur, and be more of a nuisance if this area is also *very narrow*.

ELVIS PRESLEY – WIDE HEALTH & ENERGY REGION

As may be expected, those whose Health and Energy Region is *wide* have reserves of stamina and energy that enable them to stay up for nights in a row, if required. These are, or could be, the party-loving types or those who do best at examinations by cramming in the facts the night before they sit. They can, too – if their sex drive is keen – tire their partners by their energy.

Alertness, perception and discernment are qualities admired by the masters of Siang Mien who cannot hide their disapproval of inattentive people and those whose concentration is limited in scope. Their strongest displeasure is reserved for those who drop off to sleep; they call them dopey-faced people, best recognised by the giveaway *very pointed eye tips* by the bridge of the nose.

Whether drunkenness is the cause of drowsiness or not, the Siang Mien masters advise those who want to give up, or reduce, their drink intake to 'look at a drunken person when they themselves are sober'.

HAIR ON BRIDGE OF NOSE

Sometimes the eyebrows extend into this region. *Hair* at this point evinces certain troublesome characteristics: these people get depressed easily, and are liable to imaginary illnesses and problems. Many take offence easily, too.

Those whose *eyebrows join* in the middle and who have *hair growing* in the Health and Energy Region are likely to be both ungenerous and easily offended.

8. Love Region

The Love Region is the area under the eyes, and continues on from the ends of the eyes to the hairline.

Most of the earliest masters of Siang Mien saw no connection between love and marriage. It was a time when marriages were arranged by parents, and love was not a consideration.

'Parents know best' was the accepted attitude, and if love developed after marriage, so much the better. The japonica later became known as the Love Tree, recognised as such after a hapless lady threw herself over a precipice rather than allow the emperor – who had slain her husband – to take her to his castle. The legend states that japonica trees grew from the grave of the lady and her husband, entwining their branches to symbolise married happiness, even in death.

Though arranged marriages are banned in China today, many parents still put pressure on their children to marry a particular person; this is more common in rural areas where four-fifths of the one billion population live. But even in these regions there is more talk of love, brought about in part by the influx of tourists.

The area under the eyes is the region which tells most about love. If it is *pinkish or luminous* all is well, and the relationship is going smoothly.

LINES UNDER EYES

It was not until early this century that Siang Mien masters acknowledged that broken hearts were possible, diagnosing *each line under the eyes* as a lost love. Modern interpreters of Siang Mien attribute these lines not only to heartbreaks, but also to serious disappointments in friendships and family relationships.

INDENTATIONS AT OUTER ENDS OF EYES

An *indentation at the outer ends* of the eyes, that is, a hollow area where the bone is concave, is a characteristic of those who are unable to agree with the maxim that a marriage partner should be for life.

Few, however, would openly admit their belief that it is virtually impossible to find in one person all that is needed for a relationship lasting a lifetime: loyalty, patience, mental and physical compatibility, and a similar or complementary outlook on wealth, friendship, and humour. Some concede that they themselves are not sufficiently equipped to satisfy one person for a lifetime, either.

This could be seen to be a Siang Mien verdict in favour of polygamy, as was the custom in ancient China and even this century, but the most modern Siang Mien interpretation is that those with a distinct indentation at the ends of the eyes set themselves high standards, and are difficult to satisfy in marriage.

Noticeable *bags under the eyes* are deemed adversely to affect one's fortune. But, a *fleshy* area here is an indication that this person has, or could have, bright and intelligent children, though they are likely to be mischievious.

DUKE ELLINGTON – BAGS UNDER EYES

Women who have *sunken or bluish* areas under the eyes should, advise the masters of Siang Mien, take special care of their health during pregnancy.

Crows' feet developing in the Love Region of those *under thirty-five* tell the world that these people are easily irritated by the family. In many cases they are highly resentful of the role expected of them by a lover or by the family – as breadwinner, or the person on whom many responsibilities fall.

PRESIDENT RONALD REAGAN
– CROWS' FEET

Lines, including crows' feet, that appear in the Love Region are normal, according to Siang Mien. Whether we like them or not, lines are a sign of ageing, and there is little, or nothing, that can be done to prevent their development.

Plastic surgery does not interest today's students of Siang Mien because crows' feet will return sooner or later. However, it was an ancient Chinese belief in some families that by covering the face permanently with a veil and thereby protecting the skin from light, the incidence of wrinkles would be reduced.

Few men or women would contemplate such a drastic step today, not even the most vain or the most ardent seekers of eternal youth.

Siang Mien does not link sexuality to the Love Region. The sex drive is revealed by the Mouth (Chapter VIII), Chin (XI), Ears – especially the Lobes (IX), Eyebrows (V), Eyes (VI), and even by Moles (XII).

CHAPTER XIV
Ten Famous Faces

THE QUEEN MOTHER

Those who do not know about Siang Mien, the Chinese art of reading character and personality from faces, depend on their intuition to 'tell' them if someone they have met is worthwhile.

Sometimes these first impressions are right, but more often they are not. And even if they are, those who are unable to practise Siang Mien do not know why they are right.

Most British people have a feeling that the Queen Mother is kind, the type of grandmother who is good to everyone. Siang Mien confirms this up to a point, principally because of the shape of her face. Although this type of face – Bucket face – sounds quite unflattering, those with such a face are kind and patriotic. They also have an awareness of their own importance.

Anyone involved in a close physical or emotional relationship with someone with a Bucket face can never be certain what is going on in the mind of this person, for the

Bucket-faced man or woman holds a little in reserve all the time. They are able to draw on inner strength to give the impression that all is well, even if things are going badly.

The Queen Mother's forehead is quite smooth and has a rounded sweeping hairline, a sign of friendliness and a desire to please. However, the length of her forehead in relation to the mid-section of her face (from the eyebrows to nose tip) signifies that she is often determined to get her own way, and will speak her mind if someone annoys her, or challenges her values and opinions.

Such a rounded forehead with smoothly sloping sides belongs to someone who inherits intelligence and common sense from her parents. Yet, a flat Memory Band coupled with a rounded top half of her forehead together suggest that while she is logical, her memory has never been among her strongest points.

Such pale eyebrows indicate dexterity and ability to cope with practical matters. This is the face of a practical person who sometimes frets if she thinks she could do something better or faster than the person entrusted to do a task on her behalf.

She is energetic and healthy, shown by the generous width of the Health and Energy Region situated at the bridge of the nose. Through noble birth, she has never been in financial difficulties, but it is true that anyone who has a plump nose such as hers with narrow nostrils, plus large ear lobes can expect money, and the making of it, not to be a serious problem in life.

The inner circle of her ears is wide and rounded – indicating that she is passionate in her affections.

The Queen Mother is blessed with having plump cheeks; so was Queen Victoria. Such people not only keep their youthful looks longer than those with prominent cheek-bones, but also find that very few people ever get the better of them.

Despite two Worry Creases (between the eyebrows) and a series of parallel lines between her eyes, the Queen Mother is an optimist, a fact reinforced by her upward turning mouth.

PRINCESS DIANA

The chances of becoming famous before the age of thirty are increased if the ears stand above the line of the eyebrows. Princess Diana has just such ears, although they are usually concealed beneath her thick hair.

Those with high ears who also have eyes of different sizes will have a sudden upturn of fortune that lifts them above the ordinary run of life; the princess's left eye is indeed smaller than her right. It is also a notable fact that people who have eyes of different sizes are very often those who have step-parents, as Princess Diana has.

Her right eye is Dragon shaped, revealing that she is brave and good company. The other eye is a Peacock shape, a feature associated with those who can be charming, but who are capable of unnerving jealousy if the object of their love or desire slips from their grasp.

It reinforces these observations that the princess has thin eyelashes, which tell us that, although she is normally placid and cool, she also has a sharp temper.

Until she slimmed down after her marriage, the princess's cheeks were fleshy and well-padded, and they would have acted as a buffer against anyone trying to take advantage of her. But, naturally, face-readings change as the face itself changes, so it has to be said that now she, like anyone else with sunken rather than plump cheeks, is less able to parry the unwelcome plans others may have to make use of her.

Hers is a Jade-shaped face, an auspicious shape that contributes to its owner's willpower and strength of character. This shape belongs to many whose early life has been marred by unhappy events. It is during such times that the determination to overcome setbacks takes shape. Though it is not always obvious, Jade people are tough. Her chin is strong and rounded and protrudes, and is a further pointer to her ability to weather storms and adversity.

A line runs from the inner eye across her left cheek. It is still faint because she is young, but it warns against the possibility of being used by others trying to attain power or

influence. It also hints there will be periods of disharmony at home after she has reached thirty.

Because the measurement of the top part of her face (from hairline to the top of the eyebrows) is shorter than the lower part of her face (from nose tip to chin), Princess Diana is more a do-er than a thinker, more practical than intellectual. The smooth curve of her eyebrows shows that she has a good deal of common sense, though the presence of hairs in her eyebrows that grow downward (instead of upward or sideways) reveals that the princess is immature and sometimes finds herself at odds with her family, friends, and even life itself.

Her well-concealed nostrils and a rather tight notch just above the ear lobes together show that she values money and will not give to anyone she considers does not merit her generosity.

MARGARET THATCHER

Margaret Thatcher has Triangle eyes, which belong to those who expect, and get, loyalty from friends and colleagues. Anyone who opposes or disagrees with the views of anyone with such eyes must expect to be silenced by a single, withering look. Those with Triangle eyes like everyone to agree with them. They are clever, astute and ambitious, and ideally suited to a career in politics.

Her left eyebrow is triangular in shape, revealing that though sometimes lacking ideas of her own she can always improve on the suggestions of others. Triangle eyebrows are clues to the acutely decisive nature of those who have them.

Like Greta Garbo, Margaret Thatcher has a high nose with a prominent bone. This reveals that she is rarely afraid of solitude, even craving it if her peace is threatened. A person with such a nose has to work harder than most to make a marriage succeed.

The groove located between the base of her nose and the centre of the upper lip points to a number of unresolved childhood problems which contribute to difficulty in totally relaxing; she is always alert to challenge. Those whose cheekbones are the widest part of the face, as are hers, find that throughout life many people are envious of them.

Her forehead, with its uneven hairline and hair growing on the sides at the Parental Region and the Pulse Points, tells that she has few close friends and, above all, that she trusts her own judgment better than anyone else's. Tiny indents below the corners of the mouth reveal that she is loth to delegate responsibilities to others, but being a realist, recognises that she must.

When she smiles her gums are usually visible – a sign of conflicting attitudes to giving: one moment she is generous, at other times she can be mean. When her mouth is in repose a straight line forms where her lips meet, signifying that she will do her very best to keep personal promises.

A final word about the face shape: this face is a combination of the Jade face and the King face. Those with Jade faces are durable and have a strong will to survive. Early life for many was marred by being undervalued by others and many were born poor. With such a background, many with Jade faces seek to make the most of every opportunity; they are tough, and able to overcome setbacks.

The King face is associated with leadership, and those who accept the challenge to lead find that their gift is heightened by natural militancy, toughness, and persistence. They do not give up easily, nor do they suffer fools gladly. Life with a King husband or wife is often turbulent, and requires much patience and understanding.

Elizabeth Taylor

There are two vital clues to the enigma of this beautiful face. First of all there are small indents below the corners of her mouth, representing her reticence, sometimes refusal, to trust others because above all she believes in herself and her own judgment. Vital clue number two: anyone who has this facial characteristic, and whose mid-face (from eyebrows to nose tip) is longer than the forehead, is a very determined person, bent on getting her own way in anything she considers vital to her welfare or well-being.

For further evidence of her determination and will-power look closely at her ears. The left ear (seen clearly in this photograph) shows a very prominent inner circle, standing so high that it actually conceals the outer circle, or rim, of her ear. That she is generous in love and friendship to those she respects is apparent to anyone practising Siang Mien, the Chinese art of face-reading, from the size of the notch which is situated immediately above the ear lobe; hers is wide (a small or narrow one is a tell-tale sign of a mean person).

Her penchant for 'collecting' husbands could be foreseen from the presence of very small indentations at the outer corners of the eyes. No one possessing these subscribes to the maxim that 'a marriage partner should be for life'.

Her eyes are large and Dragon-shaped, the best type of eyes one can have, for not only are they the most powerful and beautiful shape of all, but indicate that their owner is innovative, brave and generous. Although the look, or gaze, of her eyes is sensuous, it also reveals earthiness, fulsomeness, and ability to respond in a practical, down-to-earth way to people and events around her.

This photograph, and those taken when she was a teen-ager without cosmetic aids, show the perfect eyebrow shape, representing clear-mindedness, foresight and pur-posefulness.

Look closely at the line where her lips touch and you will see a near-straight line, showing that she tries to keep her word. Her teeth are even and well-shaped, pointers of a person who learns fast and is eager for new experiences. She is prepared to take risks. Her type of lower lip (thicker than the top) suggests succinctness in thought and deed, and a capacity to astonish people by unexpected, to-the-point comments, some of which could unsettle those lack-ing confidence. These lips also show voluptuousness and inventiveness in love-making.

In recent years Elizabeth Taylor's chin has grown heavier – which is purely a sign of good living.

JOAN COLLINS

This is not just a pretty face, but one which radiates seductiveness and resilience – a formidable duo of qualities. The eyes and eyebrows are the pointers to Joan Collins's sensuality and seductiveness.

Take the eyebrows first. The natural line of growth, as shown clearly in this photograph, forms the New Moon shape. Siang Mien, the Chinese art of reading faces, reveals that the female owner of this type of eyebrow is liable to

intense and sensational physical passion.

Siang Mien identifies the look, or gaze, in her eyes as the Sensuous Look, which is the look which most resembles 'bedroom eyes'. These are the eyes of a great lover who not only arouses the opposite sex, but finds throughout life that women envy her and wish they could be like her.

Her eyes are Tiger-shaped, belonging to those who can see and plan ahead. Once they have sighted their quarry, they will lie in wait for the right moment, then pounce. Those with Tiger-shaped eyes plus the Sensuous Look, or gaze, consider it important to be in control of their destiny.

The eyes provide yet more clues to her character. Being wide-set, they reveal a vigilant, watchful personality, someone who is alert to challenge yet whose fastidiousness for detail rarely permits her to rest on her laurels. She takes herself seriously, sometimes casting aside her sense of humour.

The wide nose bridge shows that her health is remarkably good, and the strong chin tells that, barring accidents, her old age will be prosperous.

That she makes contact easily with acquaintances is shown by the broad, curved sweep of her hairline (just discernible in this photograph). Yet, this face shape, known as the Fire face (widest at the forehead with sloping sides tapering to the chin) belongs to someone who is very sensitive and liable to make mistakes in the choice of partners for intimate, long-term relationships. The Fire person is quick to learn, bright and ambitious.

The mouth reveals a lot about Joan Collins. It is quite large, the lower lip slightly thicker than the top lip, and a wavy line forms where the lips join when the mouth is in repose. These qualities together tell that she inspires confidence in others by being able to communicate easily with them.

However, when she smiles her gums show, which informs the Siang Mien observer that here is someone whose generosity fluctuates, though when she is in a generous mood, she is very generous indeed.

PAUL McCARTNEY

The most remarkable thing about the face of Paul McCartney is the way his mouth and chin have altered since his youth. When a face-reading is made by the Chinese method of Siang Mien, the character traits discerned reveal the truth about that person at the time of the reading.

Look at the inset photograph of Paul McCartney when he was a young Beatle. The mouth is small – the sign of an appealing and creative lover. But most fascinating of all, his chin has a distinct groove, or small cleft, indicating that here is a young man who enjoys the limelight.

Paul McCartney is in his forties now. The mouth corners turn down more, signalling that he is more pensive than before, and has even become more pessimistic. The bottom lip is slightly thicker than the top, an indicator of someone who has a gift for entertaining other people; many actors and comedians have such a lower lip.

His chin is squarer now, a sign of leadership qualities, and the small cleft is less noticeable, showing that he craves the limelight less, preferring to lead a more private life with time to do things in his own way.

For a while he used to wear a beard, which was more scant than bushy and had some bald patches. This type of beard tells the Siang Mien observer that Paul McCartney might well have been better suited to living in a bygone age, one which would have appealed more to his values and aspirations.

His nose tells us a lot. The very wide Health and Energy Region at the bridge of the nose discloses that he has enormous energy and workaholic tendencies. The round tip reflects his huge creativity and artistry, and the slightly flaring nostrils show that though a spender, he also values the power of money and is generous only to those whom he loves or who appeal to his sense of values. This last observation is reinforced by the smallness of the notch situated just above his ear lobes.

His eyebrows are nearly perfect – rounded at the beginning, arched, and tapering to a point. Such eyebrows belong to those who are inventive, clever, ambitious and able to realise their ambitions. As with the late John Lennon, most of Paul McCartney's eyebrow roots are visible, indicating that not only can he cope with criticisms made against him, but that anyone who may feel hurt, or angered, by him will actually respect him.

His eyes are deep-set, so few people really know the true Paul McCartney. He values his privacy, and there are times when he wonders about the future of the world.

Although his fleshy ear lobes slant towards his mouth, thereby promising a comfortable life in old age, anyone who has moles on the chin or jaw – as he has – ought to value his friends, otherwise old age will be lonely.

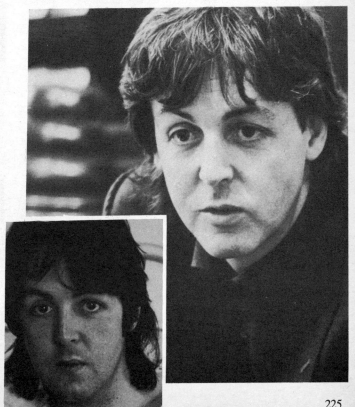

PAUL NEWMAN

Paul Newman's clear blue eyes with single lids emit a magnetic power. His face has elements of the King shape, which is generally associated with toughness, confidence and leadership skills. His chin is squarish and powerful. The combination of these eyes with such facial characteristics indicates a person who could, if he chose, exercise enormous power over others, even to the point of controlling their fortunes and destiny.

This combination of facial characteristics also belongs to those who do not, and will not, suffer fools gladly. In fact, they try to avoid the company of people who are pretentious or boring, preferring instead to mix with 'soulmates' or those who represent what they consider to be a worthwhile challenge. They are competitive, so winning is an absolute.

They do, however, have a conscience, but try to hide this through fear of being thought weak or negative. In order to conceal their true feelings, many indulge in practical jokes, quips, or humour to deflect attention from the true issue.

A fascinating aspect about Paul Newman's face is the almost equal measurements of the three zones: forehead (hairline to top of eyebrows), mid-section from eyebrows to nose tip, and the lower face (nose tip to chin). This shows that he is – in almost equal amounts – extrovert, introvert, and a man of stamina.

The small groove that runs between the base of his nose and the centre of his upper lip reveals childhood stress when he felt that 'grown-ups' did not understand him. Those who experience this often have difficulty forming lasting friendships in adulthood, but when they do they are the best sort of friends to have.

There is a distinct slope between his Life Region and Health and Energy Region, that is, from the area between his eyebrows to the bridge of the nose. This is frequently possessed by those for whom a good opportunity presents itself around their mid-twenties which, if grabbed, will quickly lead to success in their chosen career. Furthermore, his ears are higher than average, reaching slightly above the level of his eyebrows, a sign common in those who achieve fame before the age of 30. (Paul Newman was signed up by Hollywood at 27.)

The fleshy lower chin reveals a keen sex drive, yet this is not the face of one who especially welcomes a sex symbol image. As the proportions of the three zones of his face show (described in paragraph 4) he is, after all, a reflective man who needs privacy, and his features are those of a man who wants to succeed on his own terms.

RONALD REAGAN

The most striking features about this man are his ears, which are low and reach down well below the level of his nose tip. This is a sign of a late developer who achieves more after middle-age than in his youth. He is indeed the oldest man ever to have been elected President of the United States.

His ears are also long, signalling that not only does he know who is trying to get the better of him, but he has the knack of identifying who is worth cultivating as a useful friend.

One side of Ronald Reagan's forehead is slightly higher than the other, a feature that is associated with those whose childhood has been particularly troubled. The President's forehead also recedes (easily seen in profile), which tells the world that he is not a deep thinker. The forehead is narrow and shorter in length than the lower part of his face from nose tip to chin, revealing that his actions and reactions tend to be more instinctive than logical.

Some wisps of hair grow on the sides of the forehead at the Pulse Points, a sign of a self-made, hard-working person. Hair growing in this area also shows that, despite his often jocular appearance he is, deep down, less self-assured than he would like others to know. That his eyes slant down also confirms this.

His smile is angled and in repose his mouth is off-centre. Together, these features indicate that this man is not as guileless as many of his critics say, and that although he enjoys the image of a decent, straightforward guy he is much cleverer and more astute than many would suspect.

Ronald Reagan's eyebrows are close to his eyes and the bone structure immediately above the eyebrows is rather prominent. This combination of facial characteristics is associated with those who are disappointed with lack of success early in life; no doubt his Hollywood film career was not the complete success that he had hoped for. Although his eyebrows are also quite thick, the roots are visible, evidence that even those who may feel hurt by his occasional angry outbursts do, however, respect him.

His is a money-making nose: quite large, rather wide, and nostrils that barely show when seen full-face. Moles near his top lip tell us that he enjoys food, but probably gets indigestion.

A mole situated halfway between his right eyebrow and hairline shows that he is a good husband, but tiny indents at the outer ends of his eyes reveal that he would not agree with the maxim that a marriage partner has to be for life.

JOHN MCENROE

Some faces reveal their secrets more easily than others. John McEnroe's mouth gives away the secrets of his face, for a mouth that pouts like this tells the world that this is a person governed by changing moods and bouts of 'highs' and 'lows'. (There is a profile view of him on page 145 which shows his pout very clearly.)

Such a person sulks, and has either to be rapidly humoured out of a bad mood, or left alone until the mood passes, which may take a long time. Anyone who wants to live, or get on well, with a person who sulks must know which plan of action is better.

The keys to John McEnroe's success lie in his extraordinary eyes and forehead. Just above his eyebrows is a prominent bone structure, which those skilled in Siang Mien, the Chinese art of reading character in faces, will recognise as meaning that here is an extremely intuitive man, able to

sense things even before they happen. Anyone lucky to have a 'band of intuition', as this prominent bone structure is called, is a fast thinker and has quick reflexes.

His eyes are what Siang Mien identifies as Tiger-shaped, further evidence of his being able to anticipate the moves of his 'quarry', even before his opponent has made a move, which is a marvellous gift for a sportsman to have. His eyes are rather deep-set, a feature associated with someone who values his privacy. In fact, those with deep-set eyes resent anyone probing or prying into their private lives.

His hairline is V-shaped and it is beginning to recede slightly. This is a warning to all with similar hairlines that, although they may get on in life, they ought never to forget that friends should be cherished, or else old age will be very lonely and unhappy.

He is impatient, as shown by the relative closeness of his eyebrows to his eyes. Those whose eyebrows are close to the eyes and who also have a well-developed band of intuition, as he does, are extremely ambitious, but ofen find that their temperament is such that, being easily irritated, they do not achieve the goal which means most to them in life.

The shape of his cheekbones in relation to his jaw-line and forehead informs us that he feels a constant need to prove himself to others. The feeling that many people are envious and jealous of him can be detected in the fleshiness around the cheekbones and the fact that his face tapers towards the chin. This contributes to making him all the more edgy and competitive.

Some of his eyebrow hairs grow downward (rather than upward or sideways). which suggests that he is temperamental and still apt to find himself at odds with family, friends, and sometimes life itself. Yet, despite that famous pout his mouth does turn up at the corners, showing that he is more optimistic than his public behaviour sometimes suggests

John McEnroe has a good money-making nose: high, wide, a round tip, and narrow nostrils which barely show when viewed full-face. These are the nostrils of an adventurer.

LARRY HAGMAN

The man who plays the role of J.R. in the television series, *Dallas*, has said that he is shortsighted, so it will interest the many fans of Larry Hagman to learn that anyone who is shortsighted is sensuous and imaginative in love-making.

Anyone who has, as Larry Hagman has, a fleshy area in the middle of the chin, is endowed with a powerful sex urge. He also has a hint of a small cleft in the centre edge of his chin, a feature common among those who choose an acting career. This is a sign that its owner not only enjoys praise, but may even crave the spotlight.

Larry Hagman's face is essentially the Tree shape, associated with those who are able to bounce back after setbacks. Tree-faced people are resourceful, and are great protectors of their dependants and property. They hate to be trapped in a boring or unrewarding job, so will take risks and try new experiences in their keenness to put their skills to the test.

A flat patch in the middle of his forehead warns that his career will be uneven, with some good years mixed with leaner ones. But, he is lucky to have a squarish chin, which signals that if ever he chose a career where leadership skills are required, he could be extremely successful.

His eyebrows are neater at the beginning near the bridge of the nose than they are at the ends. This shows that he is an 'ideas man', someone with a lot of imagination who is better at originating ideas than seeing them through.

His nose tip is round and plump, and the nostrils are supported by fleshy sides; this reveals that he is not especially adventurous with money, yet he will spend generously on those whom he loves, or respects.

A rather narrow Health and Energy Region across the bridge of the nose denotes health problems, but the expression and look in his eyes – confident, clear, direct – hints at a sense of fun and playfulness that will help him overcome difficulties.

His ears are very interesting for they are thick, long, and the inner circle and lobes are bumpy. Together, these features indicate someone who instinctively helps those who deserve help, and uncannily senses when someone is trying to take advantage of him. Anyone who underestimates Larry Hagman would quickly feel his displeasure.

A mole just above the Pulse Points on his forehead indicates that he is a good husband.

Photograph Acknowledgments

The publishers and author wish to thank the following for their kind permission to reproduce the illustrations: the National Portrait Gallery for the photographs on pages 48, 50 and 91; the Keystone Press Agency for the photograph on page 202; Popperfoto for the photographs on pages 44, 58 (top) 79, 165 and 170; the Mansell Collection for the photographs on pages 85, 107 and 131; Golden Communications for the photograph on page 92; Syndication International for the photograph on page 145; Camera Press for the photographs on page 57, page 58 (bottom) (Patrick Lichfield), page 214 (Norman Parkinson), page 217 (Snowdon), page 218 (Bernard Charlton), page 220 (Curt Gunther), page 222 (Jerry Watson), 225 (bottom) (Roma Press Photo), page 226 (HPS), page 228 (Alan Oxley), page 230 (Hilary Andrews), page 233 (Jerry Watson), page 43 (SAYE), page 47 (Vivienne of London), page 53 (Kurt Wyss), page 190 (top), page 190 (bottom), *The Times*, London, page 193 (Richard Slade), page 198 (Norman Parkinson), page 202 (Karsh of Ottawa), page 206 (Sven Simon), page 210, page 211 (Michael Evans), page 70 (David Steen), page 76, page 77 (Jacques Haillot, *L'Express*), page 82 (Julien Quideau, *L'Express*), page 87 (Leon Herschtritt), page 88 (Tom Hanley), page 93 (left and right), page 96 (Brian Aris), page 98, page 104 (John Garrett), page 105 (MG/Johnson), page 111 (Max Ehlert), page 113 (Sam Levin), page 114 (ASP), page 120 (Jean Ker, Ilphot), page 121 (Jerry Watson), page 122 (David Bailey), page 124, page 125, page 128 (Jerry Watson), page 129 (Cecil Beaton), page 132 (Symil Kumar Dutt), page 133 (Endre Friedmann, copyright Interfoto MTI + Hungary), page 136 (L. Schiller), page 139 (Horst Tappe), page 142 (John Bryson), page 144 (Ralph Crane), page 146, page 147 (Gerald Buthaud), page 149 (David Bailey), page 150, page 155 (Alan Davidson), page 156 (Herb Snitzer), page 41 (Sven Simon), page 158 (Snowdon), page 159 (top, TPS/BASSANO), page 159 (bottom), page 161 (Jon Blau), page 162 (Jerry Watson), page 163 (IPPA), page 169 (top, BASSANO), page 169 (inset), page 171 (Ralph Crane), page 177 (Karsh of Ottawa), page 54 (John Bryson), page 179, page 181 (left, Czechoslovak News Agency), page 181 (right, Albert Clack), page 185 and The Times Newspaper the photograph on page 225 (top).